MathFlare

Name: _______________________

Class: __________

Teacher: _______________________

Introduction

As parents and educators, we recognize the pivotal role mathematics plays in shaping a child's academic journey and future success. Yet, the path to mathematical proficiency can often seem daunting, fraught with challenges and complexities. That's where the transformative power of MathFlare Workbooks shine through, illuminating the way forward with clarity, precision, and purpose.

Introducing MathFlare Workbooks – a beacon of guidance, a testament to excellence, and a catalyst for achievement. Crafted with meticulous care and expertise, MathFlare Workbooks stand as paragons of educational excellence, designed to nurture young minds, ignite a passion for learning, and develop a deep-rooted understanding of mathematical concepts.

Picture this: your child eagerly delves into the pages of Mathflare Workbook, greeted by a step-by-step guide illuminated with vivid examples that demystify complex mathematical concepts. With each turn of the page, they embark on a journey of discovery, encountering thoughtfully curated practice questions that reinforce learning and hone problem-solving skills. And when they unveil the answers to those very questions, a sense of accomplishment blossoms within them – a tangible reward for their hard work and dedication.

But MathFlare Workbooks are more than just tools for learning; they are pathways to comprehension, fostering a deep-seated understanding of mathematical concepts through a sequential, logical flow. From fundamental principles to advanced problem-solving strategies, every chapter builds upon the last, ensuring a robust foundation upon which future knowledge can be constructed.

As parents, we yearn for nothing more than to see our children thrive, to witness the spark of inspiration ignited within them as they conquer academic challenges with confidence and poise. MathFlare Workbooks serve as partners in this noble endeavor, offering not just practice questions, but the keys to unlocking a world of opportunity.

And for teachers, MathFlare Workbooks stand as invaluable allies in the quest to cultivate mathematical proficiency in the classroom. With answers readily available, instructors can focus on guiding and nurturing their students, confident in the knowledge that MathFlare Workbooks provide a solid framework upon which to build.

In the pages of MathFlare Workbooks, we find not just the promise of academic excellence, but the seeds of a brighter tomorrow. So let us embrace the power of mathematics, let us champion the journey of learning, and let us pave the way for a generation of young minds poised to shape the world. With MathFlare Workbooks as our guide, the possibilities are infinite, and the future, bright.

Table of Contents

MathFlare
Grade 2
MATH WORKBOOK
Step by Step Guide and Essential Practice with Answers
Addition Subtraction
Multiplication
Place Value and Expanded Notations
Geometry
MathFlare Publishing

MathFlare
Grade 2-3
MATH WORKBOOK
Step by Step Guide and Essential Practice with Answers
Addition Subtraction
Multiplication and Division
Place Value and Expanded Notations
Geometry
MathFlare Publishing

MathFlare
Grade 3
MATH WORKBOOK
Step by Step Guide and Essential Practice with Answers
Multiplication and Division
Decimals
Place Value and Expanded Notations
Fractions and Geometry
MathFlare Publishing

MathFlare
Grade 1
MATH WORKBOOK
Step by Step Guide and Essential Practice with Answers
Counting and Numbers
Addition and Subtraction
Place Value and Expanded Notations
Understanding Time
MathFlare Publishing

MathFlare
Grade 1-2
MATH WORKBOOK
Step by Step Guide and Essential Practice with Answers
Counting and Numbers
Addition and Subtraction
Place Value and Expanded Notations
Understanding Time
MathFlare Publishing

MathFlare
Grade 3-4
MATH WORKBOOK
Step by Step Guide and Essential Practice with Answers
Addition Subtraction
Multiplication Division
Place Value and Expanded Notations
Fractions and Geometry
MathFlare Publishing

MathFlare
Grade 4
MATH WORKBOOK
Step by Step Guide and Essential Practice with Answers
Addition Subtraction
Multiplication Division
Place Value and Expanded Notations
Fractions and Geometry
MathFlare Publishing

MathFlare
Grade 4-5
MATH WORKBOOK
Step by Step Guide and Essential Practice with Answers
Multiplication Division
Place Value and Expanded Notations
Fractions and Geometry
Unit Conversion
MathFlare Publishing

MathFlare
MATH
WORKBOOK
5
Step by Step Guide
and Essential Practice
with Answers
Multiplication
Division
Place Value and
Expanded
Notations
Fractions
and Geometry
Unit
Conversion
MathFlare Publishing

MathFlare
MATH
WORKBOOK
5-6
Step by Step Guide
and Essential Practice
with Answers
Multiplication
Division
Place Value and
Expanded
Notations
Fractions
and Geometry
Units and
Statistics
MathFlare Publishing

MathFlare
MATH
WORKBOOK
6
Step by Step Guide
and Essential Practice
with Answers
Integers and
Statistics
Arithmetic and
Pre-Algebra
Fractions
and Geometry
Ratio and
Percentage
MathFlare Publishing

MathFlare
MATH
WORKBOOK
6-7
Step by Step Guide
and Essential Practice
with Answers
Arithmetic and
Pre-Algebra
Ratio, Percent
Proportion
Geometry
Statistics
MathFlare Publishing

MathFlare
MATH
WORKBOOK
7
Step by Step Guide
and Essential Practice
with Answers
Pre-Algebra
Ratio, Percent
Proportion
Geometry
Statistics
MathFlare Publishing

MathFlare
MATH
WORKBOOK
7-8
Step by Step Guide
and Essential Practice
with Answers
Pre-Algebra
Ratio, Percent
Proportion
Geometry and
Cartesian
Plane
Statistics
MathFlare Publishing

MathFlare
MATH
WORKBOOK
8-9
Step by Step Guide
and Essential Practice
with Answers
Pre-Algebra
Ratio, Proportion
and Percentage
Linear
Equations
Geometry and
Cartesian Plane
MathFlare Publishing

MathFlare
MATH
WORKBOOK
8
Step by Step Guide
and Essential Practice
with Answers
Pre-Algebra
Percentage
Linear
Equations
Geometry
MathFlare Publishing

Operations with Whole Numbers

Positive and negative integers are whole numbers that can represent quantities greater than zero and less than zero, respectively.

Positive Integers: Positive integers are whole numbers greater than zero. They are denoted by the numbers 1,2,3,4...

Negative Integers: Negative integers are whole numbers less than zero. They are denoted by placing a negative sign ("-") before the numbers, such as $-1,-2,-3,-4,...$

The positive integers are used to represent the number of objects, scores, etc. whereas the negative integers can be used to represent debt, losses, temperatures below freezing points, etc.

Let's solve some problems:

1. $6 - (-8) - 9$

- Start by simplifying within the parentheses:

$$-(-8) \text{ becomes } 8.$$

- Rewrite the expression with the simplified part:

$$6 + 8 - 9.$$

- Now perform addition and subtraction from left to right:

$$6 + 8 = 14, \text{ then } 14 - 9 = 5$$

2. $(-5) - (-3) + 10$

$$(-5) + 3 + 10$$

$$(-5) + 3 = -2, \text{ then } -2 + 10 = 8$$

Operations with Decimals

Adding Decimals

Adding decimals is like adding whole numbers, but we must align the decimal points carefully. For instance, when adding 49.88 and 45.78:

Step 1: Align the decimal points.

$$49.88$$
$$+\ 45.78$$

Step 2: Start adding from the rightmost digit (the ones place) and move to the left.

Add 8 and 8: 8 + 8 = 16. Write down 6 in the ones place and carry over 1 to the tenths place.

$$49.88$$
$$+\ 45.78$$
$$6$$

Step 3: Add the tenths place.

Add 1 (carried over from the previous step), 8, and 7: 1 + 8 + 7 = 16. Write down 6 in the tenths place and carry over 1 to the hundredths place.

$$49.88$$
$$+\ 45.78$$
$$66$$

Step 4: Continue adding digits to the left until you reach the leftmost digit:

$$49.88$$
$$+\ 45.78$$
$$9566$$

<u>Step 5: Finally, write the sum with the decimal point directly below the decimal points in the original numbers.</u>

$$49.88$$
$$+\ 45.78$$
$$95.66$$

Let's solve a problem:

$$835.68$$
$$+\ 825.29$$
$$1{,}660.97$$

Subtracting Decimals

Subtracting decimals follows a process like adding decimals, except instead of adding the numbers, we subtract them.

For example:

$$697.05$$
$$-\ 258.40$$
$$438.65$$

Multiplying Decimals

Multiplying decimals is a lot like multiplying whole numbers, but we need to be careful about where we put the decimal point in the answer.

Step 1: Start by multiplying the numbers together, just like we do with whole numbers. Ignore the decimals for now.

Step 2: Count how many decimal places there are in the numbers we're multiplying. This will tell us how many decimal places our answer should have.

Step 3: Put the decimal point in the answer by starting from the right side of the number. Move the decimal point to the left as many places as there are in the total number of decimal places.

For example, let's multiply 4.5 by 2.5:

Step 1: Multiply the numbers as if they were whole numbers:

$$25 \times 45 = 1125.$$

Step 2: There is one decimal place in 2.5 and one in 4.5, making a total of two decimal places.

Step 3: Starting from the right side of the answer, count two places to the left and put the decimal point there.

So, the final answer is 11.25.

Remember to pay close attention to where the decimal point goes in the answer.

Let's solve a problem:

$$
\begin{array}{r}
85.39 \\
\times \quad 1.44 \\
\hline
+ \;\; 34156 \\
+ \; 34156 \\
+ \; 8539 \\
\hline
= 12\,2.9616 \\
\end{array}
$$

Dividing Decimals

Dividing decimals is a lot like dividing whole numbers, but we need to be careful about placement of decimal point in the answer.

Steps to follow:

1. **Set up the division problem:** Write the dividend (the number being divided) and the divisor (the number you're dividing by) as you would in a long division problem.

$$1.7 \overline{)1.6}$$

2. **Move the decimal:** Move the decimal point to the right in the dividend and divisor by the same number of places.

$$17 \overline{)16}$$

3. **Perform the division:** Divide as you would with whole numbers.

$$
\begin{array}{r}
0\,0.9\,4 \\
17 \overline{)16} \\
-\,0 \\
\hline
16 \\
-\,0 \\
\hline
16\,0 \\
-\,15\,3 \\
\hline
7\,0 \\
-\,6\,8 \\
\hline
2
\end{array}
$$

4. **Place the decimal point:** Place the decimal point in the quotient directly above its position in the dividend.

So, the quotient is 0.94.

Let's solve another problem:

$$\begin{array}{r} 4.567 \\ 12\overline{)54.8} \\ -0 \\ \hline 54 \\ -48 \\ \hline 68 \\ -60 \\ \hline 80 \\ -72 \\ \hline 80 \\ -72 \\ \hline 8 \end{array}$$

Using the Power of 10

Using the powers of 10, 100, and 1000 makes multiplying and dividing by these numbers very convenient. Let's illustrate with examples:

Multiplying by Powers of 10:

- To multiply a number by 10, simply move the decimal point one place to the right.

$$5 \times 10 = 50$$

- To multiply a number by 100, move the decimal point two places to the right.

$$5 \times 100 = 500$$

- To multiply a number by 1000, move the decimal point three places to the right.

$$5 \times 1000 = 5000.$$

Dividing by Powers of 10:

- To divide a number by 10, simply move the decimal point one place to the left.

$$50 \div 10 = 5$$

- To divide a number by 100, move the decimal point two places to the left.

$$500 \div 100 = 5$$

- To divide a number by 1000, move the decimal point three places to the left.

$$5000 \div 1000 = 5$$

Exponents and Roots

Exponents

An exponent tells us how many times a number (called the base) is multiplied by itself. It is written as a superscript to the right of the base number. For example, in 2^3, 2 is the base and 3 is the exponent.

Rules:

1. **Product Rule**: When multiplying powers with the same base, add the exponents.

$$a^m \times a^n = a^{m+n}$$

For example:

$$2^3 = 2 \times 2 \times 2 = 8$$

$$3^2 \times 3^4 = 3^{2+4} = 3^6 = 3 \times 3 \times 3 \times 3 \times 3 \times 3 = 729$$

2. **Quotient Rule**: When dividing powers with the same base, subtract the exponents.

$$a^m \div a^n = a^{m-n}$$

For example:

$$5^3 \div 5^2 = 5^{3-2} = 5^1 = 5$$

3. **Power of a Power Rule**: When raising a power to another power, multiply the exponents.

$$(a^m)^n = a^{mn}$$

For example:

$$(2^2)^3 = 2^{2 \times 3} = 2^6 = 64$$

4. **Power of a Product Rule**: When raising a product to a power, distribute the power to each factor.

$$(ab)^n = a^n \times b^n$$

For example:

$$(2 \times 3)^2 = 2^2 \times 3^2 = 4 \times 9 = 36$$

5. **Power of a Quotient Rule**: When raising a quotient to a power, distribute the power to the numerator and denominator separately.

$$\left(\frac{a}{b}\right)^n = \frac{a^n}{b^n}$$

For example:

$$\left(\frac{4}{2}\right)^3 = \frac{4^3}{2^3} = \frac{64}{8} = 8$$

6. **Zero Exponent Rule**: Any nonzero number raised to the power of zero equals 11.

$$a^0 = 1$$

For example:

$$7^0 = 1$$

7. **Negative Exponent Rule**: A negative exponent means the reciprocal of the base raised to the positive exponent.

$$a^{-n} = \frac{1}{a^n}$$

For example:

$$2^{-3} = \frac{1}{2^3} = \frac{1}{8}$$

To evaluate expressions with exponents, we can use:

- **Repeated Multiplication**: Perform the multiplication indicated by the exponent.

- **Using the Rules of Exponents**: Apply the appropriate rule to simplify expressions involving exponents.

Square Roots

The square root of a number is a value that, when multiplied by itself, gives the original number. It's denoted by the symbol $\sqrt{\ }$.

For example, the square root of 9 is 3 because 3 * 3 = 9.

Cube Roots

The cube root of a number is a value that, when multiplied by itself twice, gives the original number. It's denoted by the symbol $\sqrt[3]{\ }$.

For example, the cube root of 8 is 2 because 2 * 2 * 2 = 8.

Operations with Mixed Numbers

Mixed numbers and improper fractions are two different ways to represent the same value of a fraction.

1. **Mixed Number:** A mixed number is a combination of a whole number and a proper fraction. For example, $2\frac{1}{3}$ is a mixed number, where 2 is the whole number part and $\frac{1}{3}$ is the fraction part.

2. **Improper Fraction:** An improper fraction is a fraction where the numerator is greater than or equal to the denominator. For example, $\frac{7}{3}$ is an improper fraction because 6 is greater than 3.

To convert a mixed number to an improper fraction, you multiply the whole number by the denominator of the fraction, add the numerator, and then write the result over the original denominator. For example:

$$2\frac{1}{3} = \frac{2 \times 3 + 1}{3} = \frac{7}{3}$$

To convert an improper fraction to a mixed number, we divide the numerator by the denominator. The quotient becomes the whole number part, and the remainder becomes the numerator of the fraction. For example:

$$\frac{7}{3} = 2\frac{1}{3}$$

Let's solve some problems:

$$2\frac{10}{20} = \frac{20 \times 2 = 40}{40 + 10 = 50} = \frac{50}{20} = \frac{5}{2}$$

$$\frac{91}{14} = \frac{91 \div 7 = 13}{14 \div 7 = 2} = 6\frac{1}{2}$$

$$13 \div 2 = 6 \text{ with a remainder of } 1$$

Mixed Numbers: Addition and Subtraction

To add or subtract mixed numbers, we follow similar steps as when adding or subtracting regular fractions. For instance:

Addition:

- Add the whole numbers: Add the whole number parts of the mixed numbers together.
- Add the fractions: Add the fractions parts of the mixed numbers together.
- Simplify (if needed): If the fraction part of the sum is an improper fraction, simplify it by converting it to a mixed number.

Subtraction:

- Subtract the whole numbers: Subtract the whole number part of the second mixed number from the whole number part of the first mixed number.
- Subtract the fractions: Subtract the fraction part of the second mixed number from the fraction part of the first mixed number.
- Simplify (if needed): If the fraction part of the difference is a negative fraction , borrow from the whole number part or simplify it by converting it to a mixed number.

Let's solve some problems:

$$3\frac{4}{8} + 7\frac{1}{3} = \frac{4}{8} + \frac{1}{3} = \frac{4\times3 + 8\times1}{8\times3} = \frac{12+8}{24} = \frac{20}{24} = 10\frac{5}{6}$$

$$3 + 7 = 10$$

$$7\frac{4}{6} - 2\frac{3}{8} = \frac{4}{6} - \frac{3}{8} = \frac{4\times8 - 6\times3}{6\times8} = \frac{32-18}{48} = \frac{14}{48} = 5\frac{7}{24}$$

$$7 - 2 = 5$$

Mixed Numbers: Multiplication and Division

To multiply or divide mixed numbers, we follow these steps:

Multiplication:

- <u>Convert the mixed numbers to improper fractions</u>: Multiply the whole number by the denominator of the fraction, then add the numerator. Write the result over the original denominator.
- <u>Multiply the fractions</u>: Multiply the numerators together to get the new numerator and multiply the denominators together to get the new denominator.
- <u>Simplify (if needed)</u>: If the result is an improper fraction, simplify it by converting it back to a mixed number.

Division:

- <u>Convert the mixed numbers to improper fractions:</u>
- <u>Invert the divisor</u>: Flip the second fraction (the one you're dividing by) so that the division becomes multiplication.
- <u>Multiply the fractions</u>: Multiply the numerators together to get the new numerator and multiply the denominators together to get the new denominator.
- <u>Simplify (if needed)</u>: If the result is an improper fraction, simplify it by converting it back to a mixed number.

Let's solve some problems:

$$1\frac{2}{4} \times 3\frac{1}{6} = \frac{3}{2} \times \frac{19}{6} = \frac{3 \times 19}{2 \times 6} = \frac{57}{12} = 4\frac{3}{4}$$

$$1 \times 4 + 2 = 6 = \frac{6}{2} = \frac{3}{2} \qquad 3 \times 8 + 1 = \frac{19}{6}$$

Multiple Operations Fractions

Fraction multiple operations involve performing multiple arithmetic operations (addition, subtraction, multiplication, division) on fractions.

We follow (PEDMAS that stands for the order of operations in arithmetic) to solve multiple operations Fractions:

1. **Parentheses:** Perform operations inside parentheses first.

2. **Exponents:** Evaluate expressions with exponents or powers.

3. **Multiplication and Division:** Perform multiplication and division from left to right.

4. **Addition and Subtraction:** Perform addition and subtraction from left to right.

For example:

Let's solve the expression: $\dfrac{3}{4} + \dfrac{1}{2} \times \dfrac{2}{3}$

Step 1: Begin by performing the multiplication operation first:

$$= \dfrac{1 \times 2}{2 \times 4} = \dfrac{2}{6} = \dfrac{1}{3}$$

Step 2: Now rewrite the expression with the result of the multiplication:

$$\dfrac{3}{4} + \dfrac{1}{3}$$

Step 3: To add fractions, find a common denominator. In this case, the least common multiple (LCM) of 4 and 3 is 12.

Step 4: Rewrite both fractions with the common denominator:

$$\dfrac{9}{12} + \dfrac{4}{12}$$

Step 5: Add the numerators together and keep the common denominator:

$$\dfrac{13}{12} = 1\dfrac{1}{12}$$

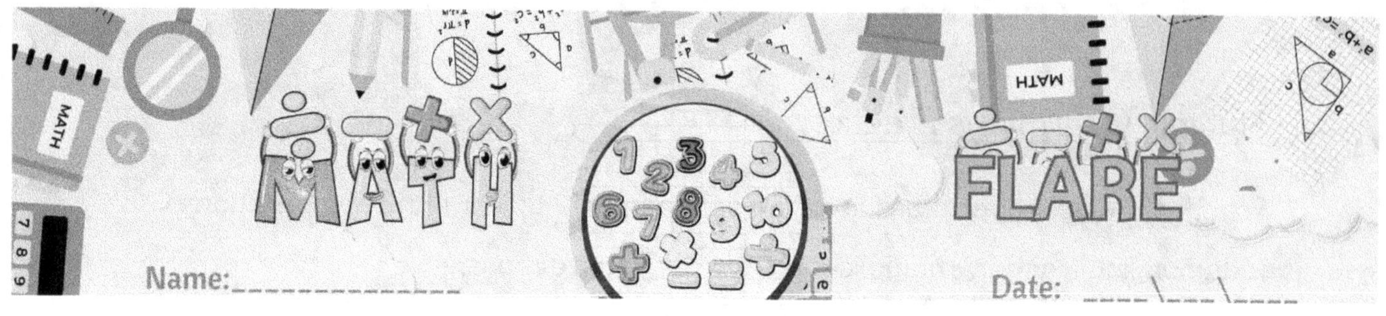

Operations with Whole Numbers

1. $5 - 7 - (6 + 5) =$

2. $1 - 8 - 2 - 8 =$

3. $(-2) + 10 + (-5) =$

4. $6 - 2 + 10 =$

5. $5 + 6 - (8 + 5) =$

6. $1 + (-6) =$

7. $4 + 3 - 4 =$

8. $3 - (7 - 6) =$

9. $3 - 8 - (4 + 3) =$

10. $2 + (-7) - 1 =$

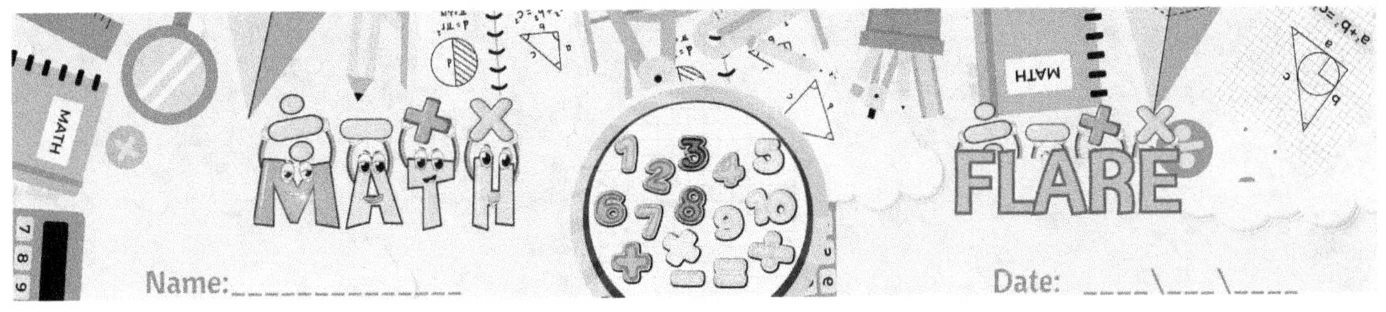

11. $(-7) + 5 + (-6) =$

12. $7 - 2 - 4 - 10 =$

13. $10 - (6 + 10) + 1 =$

14. $4 + (-4) - 5 =$

15. $9 - 8 - 2 =$

16. $7 - (1 - 5) =$

17. $2 - 5 + (-3) =$

18. $4 - (-3) =$

19. $8 - (6 + 5) - 5 =$

20. $4 - 9 + 9 =$

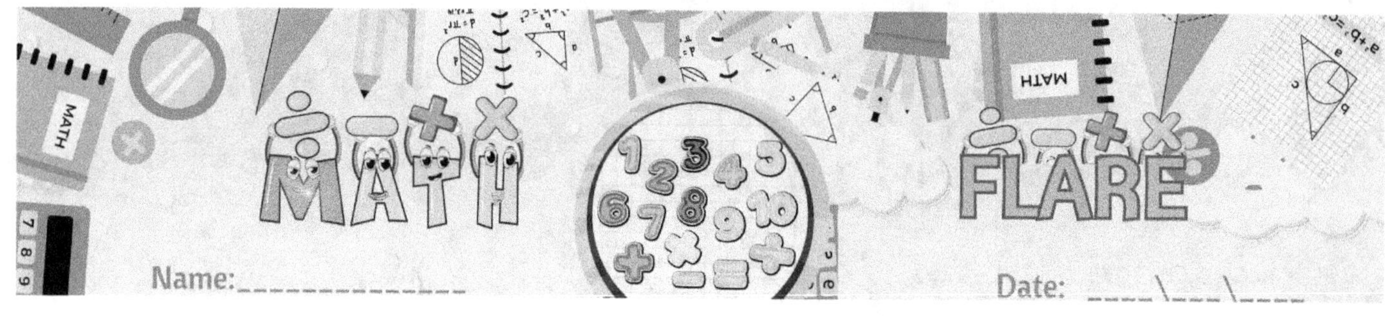

21. $8 + 5 - (5 + 5) =$

22. $(-10) + (-9) + 7 =$

23. $1 - (-2) =$

24. $6 + (-9) =$

25. $3 - (4 + 10) + 4 =$

26. $1 - (-5) =$

27. $1 - 3 + 7 =$

28. $1 - 3 + 10 =$

29. $3 + (-3) - 2 =$

30. $(-4) + (-4) + 8 =$

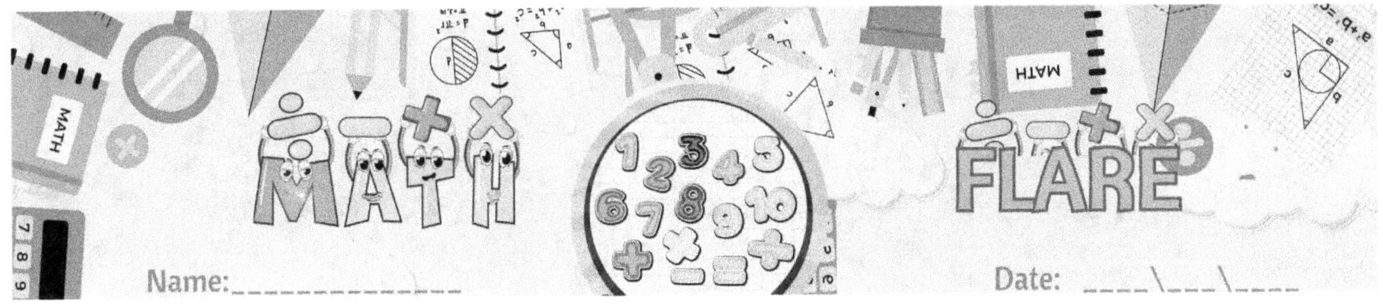

31. $(-5) + 6 =$

32. $2 - 2 - 2 - 6 =$

33. $10 - 10 + 4 =$

34. $9 + (-3) + 1 =$

35. $10 + 3 - (7 + 6) =$

36. $10 - 1 - 4 =$

37. $5 - (5 - 10) =$

38. $5 + (2 - 2) =$

39. $(-8) + 6 + (-6) =$

40. $3 + (-2) - 8 =$

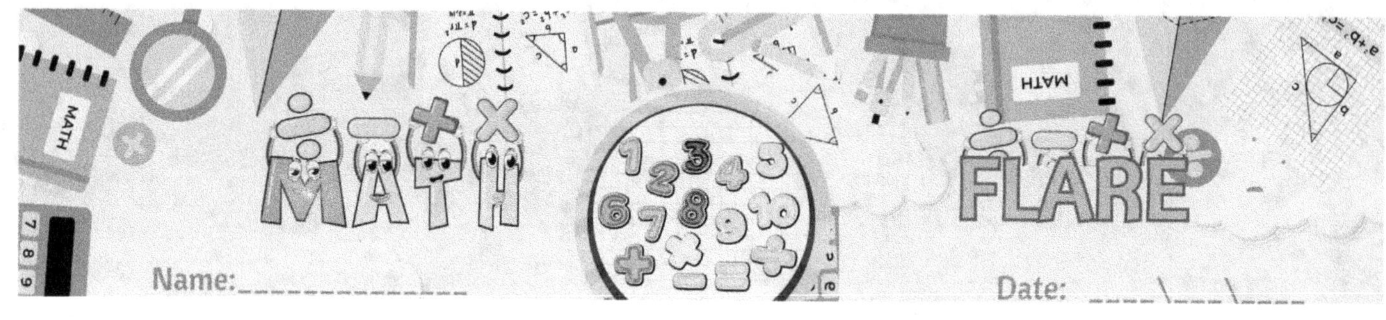

41. 5 + (− 3) − 3 =

42. 8 + (1 − 8) =

43. 2 − 2 + 4 =

44. 5 − (2 + 1) − 2 =

45. 10 + 6 − 2 =

46. 1 − 3 − 7 =

47. 4 + 2 − 1 + 10 =

48. 4 + 5 − 2 =

49. 1 − (10 + 5) + 1 =

50. 4 + 8 − (3 + 1) =

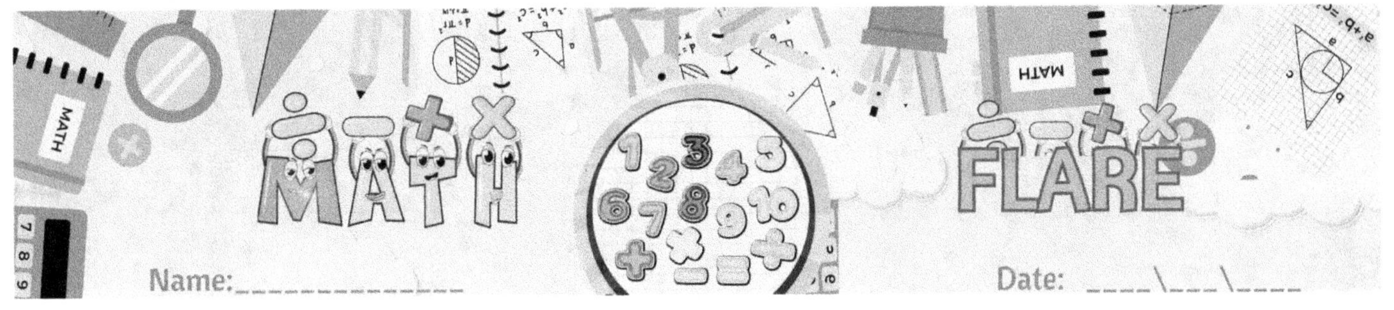

Name:______________

Date: ____________

51. $9 - (8 + 7) - 6 =$

52. $(-6) + 9 + (-8) =$

53. $10 - 10 - 10 - 4 =$

54. $9 - (-3) =$

55. $2 + (6 - 7) =$

56. $6 - 3 - (7 + 8) =$

57. $7 - (5 + 4) - 10 =$

58. $3 - (-9) - 7 =$

59. $3 - (-7) =$

60. $4 - 1 + 4 =$

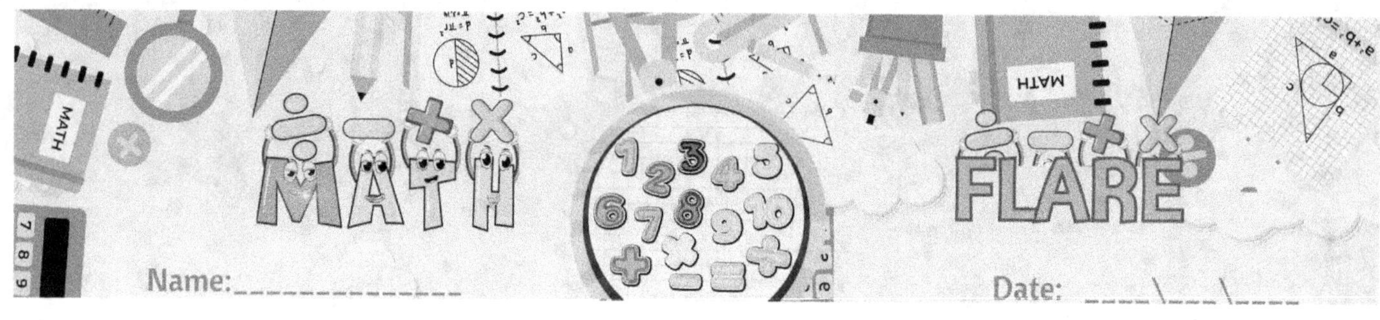

61. $9 - (2 + 2) - 9 =$

62. $6 - (5 + 7) + 8 =$

63. $7 - 3 - (1 + 10) =$

64. $1 - 6 - (10 + 9) =$

65. $4 + (8 - 6) =$

66. $2 - 2 + (- 5) =$

67. $4 + 4 - 5 =$

68. $8 - 4 - 7 =$

69. $2 + 6 - 3 =$

70. $7 + 10 - 10 + 1 =$

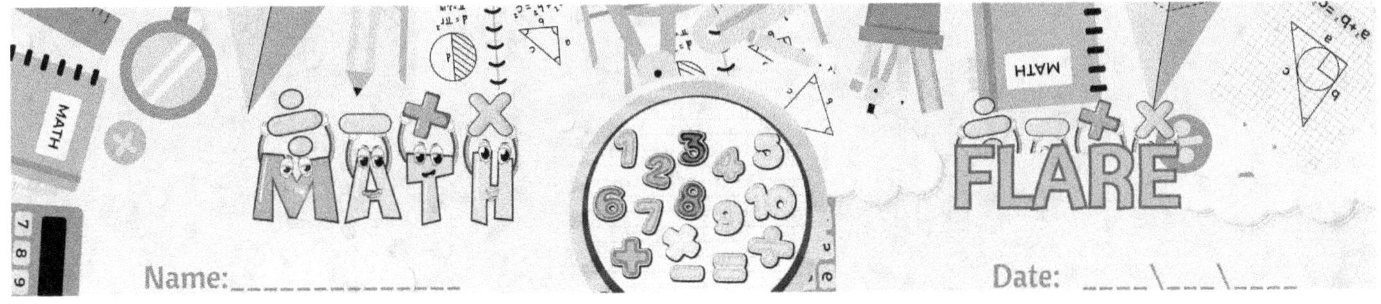

71. $(-1) + (-1) + 8 =$

72. $2 + 1 - 6 + 9 =$

73. $2 - (5 + 4) - 4 =$

74. $9 - 7 - 10 =$

75. $9 + (-9) + 10 =$

76. $9 - (10 + 2) - 5 =$

77. $8 - 8 - 4 - 9 =$

78. $(-2) + 10 =$

79. $6 + (-1) + 1 =$

80. $5 + (-1) + 1 =$

81. $6 - (-10) - 8 =$

82. $6 - 7 + 5 =$

83. $6 - (-3) - 3 =$

84. $10 + 10 - 1 =$

85. $9 + (-8) - 8 =$

86. $4 + 7 - 4 =$

87. $8 + 1 - 8 + 7 =$

88. $3 - (4 + 4) - 4 =$

89. $10 - (6 - 3) =$

90. $2 - 4 - 10 - 4 =$

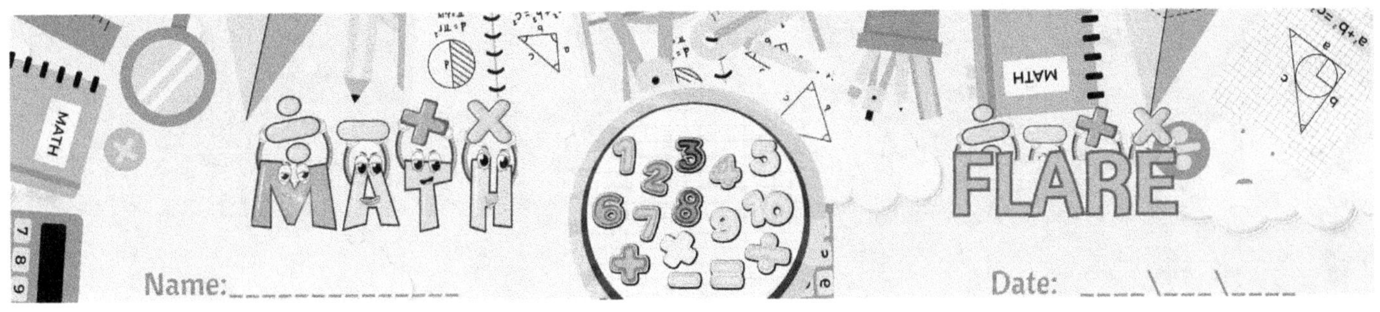

91. $9 - (1 + 1) + 1 =$

92. $3 + (- 3) - 4 =$

93. $4 - (- 9) - 2 =$

94. $9 - 8 + 4 =$

95. $10 - 5 + 3 =$

96. $3 - 5 - 8 - 7 =$

97. $1 - (- 3) =$

98. $10 - (7 - 5) =$

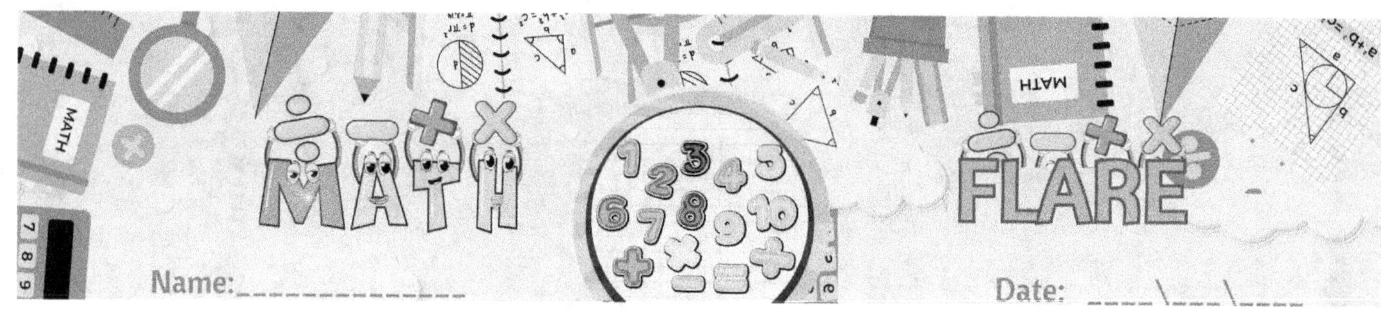

Operations with Decimals

Complete the operations.

1. $67.80 + 99.16$

2. 5.0×9.0

3. $88.08 - 67.23$

4. 3.3×5.7

5. $30.45 + 13.67$

6. $95.05 + 40.71$

7. 4.6×9.3

8. $3.6\overline{)4.1}$

9. $3.6\overline{)5.7}$

10. 1.4×6.6

11. 2.5×1.2

12. $37.96 + 73.59$

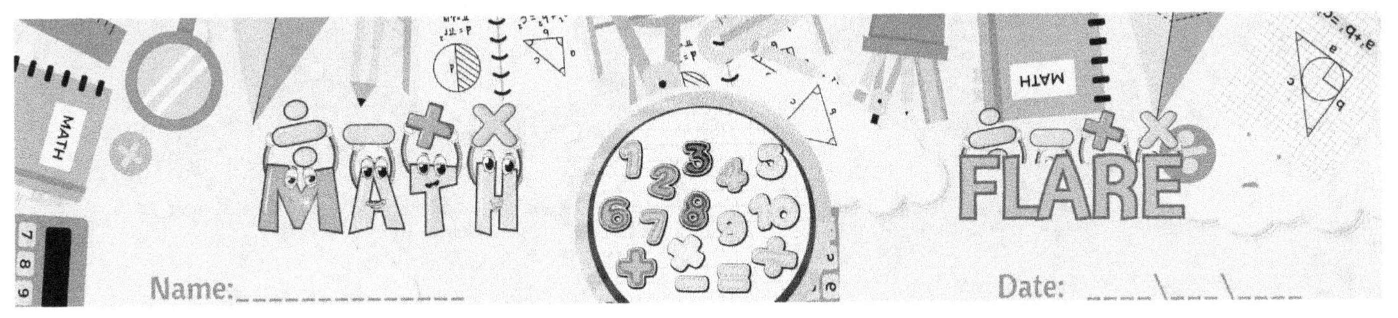

13. $$90.24 - 31.31$$

14. $$8.1\overline{)4.4}$$

15. $$1.3 \times 5.4$$

16. $$7.4 \times 7.5$$

17. $$41.68 - 29.45$$

18. $$95.21 - 38.94$$

19. $$82.30 - 16.98$$

20. $$2.3\overline{)4.2}$$

21. $$92.51 - 21.45$$

22. $$88.52 + 24.03$$

23. $$5.9 \times 2.6$$

24. $$8.8\overline{)4.0}$$

25. $$68.76 + 53.77$$

26. $$3.3 \times 9.1$$

27. $$6.1 \times 6.1$$

28. $$60.11 - 53.74$$

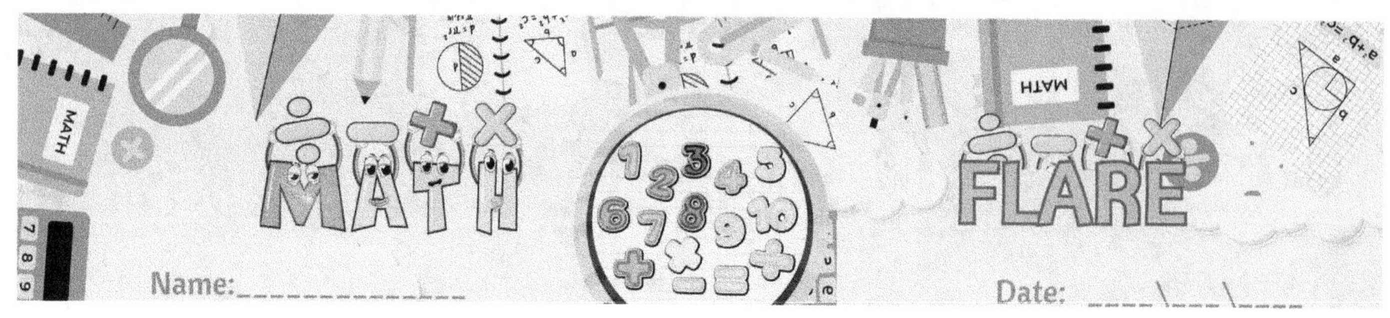

29. 5.1
   × 1.1
____

30. 22.51
   + 80.91
____

31. 4.1
   × 7.1
____

32. 8.1)‾8.1

33. 76.37
   − 42.48
____

34. 77.49
   − 28.50
____

35. 23.63
   + 78.66
____

36. 52.39
   − 43.96
____

37. 30.39
   + 48.92
____

38. 3.0
   × 2.8
____

39. 8.9)‾4.9

40. 6.1)‾9.5

41. 2.3)‾7.9

42. 89.66
   + 61.95
____

43. 7.7)‾8.8

44. 47.44
   + 26.87
____

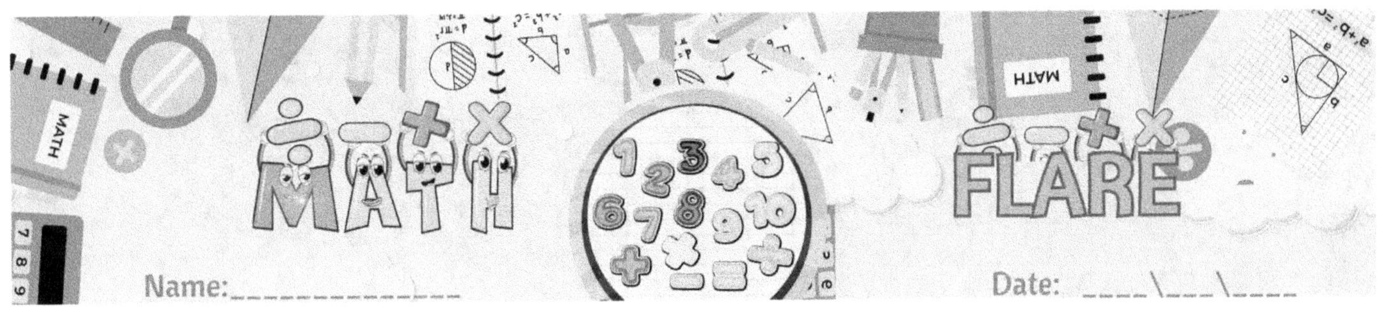

45.   19.60
  + 75.48

46. $5.3\overline{)6.1}$

47.   8.7
  × 8.8

48.   29.62
  + 81.23

49.   82.77
  + 42.29

50.   60.49
  + 16.00

51. $4.7\overline{)2.6}$

52.   71.08
  − 33.48

53.   7.0
  × 4.5

54. $4.2\overline{)4.3}$

55.   3.3
  × 9.5

56.   21.80
  + 35.83

57.   77.81
  + 82.26

58.   1.4
  × 1.5

59.   63.42
  + 60.83

60.   75.92
  − 30.15

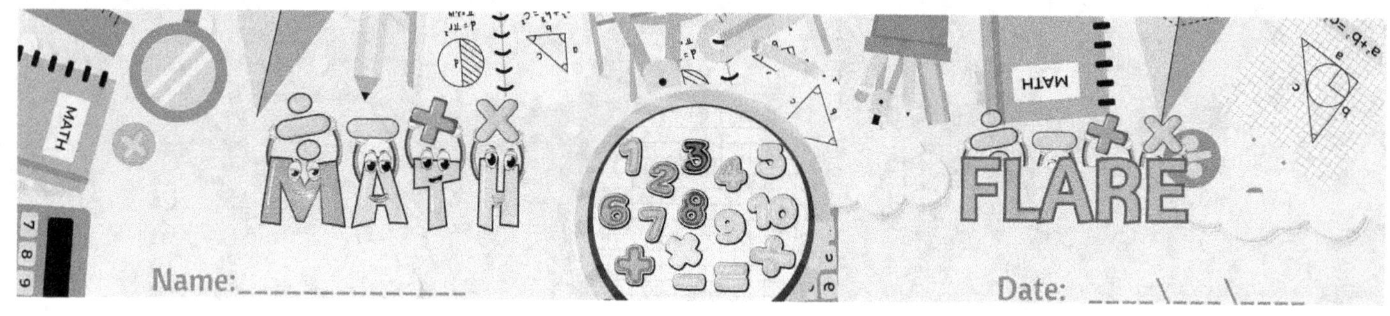

61. 1.6)4.9

62. 1.7)1.6

63. 49.62
   - 15.15

64. 1.5)8.9

65. 84.92
   - 69.43

66. 6.9)9.2

67. 61.58
   + 32.65

68. 8.8
   × 4.2

69. 7.2
   × 6.0

70. 9.4)1.6

71. 59.99
   + 49.42

72. 97.10
   + 47.58

73. 1.2
   × 3.5

74. 86.52
   - 47.80

75. 71.56
   - 68.53

76. 83.94
   + 46.68

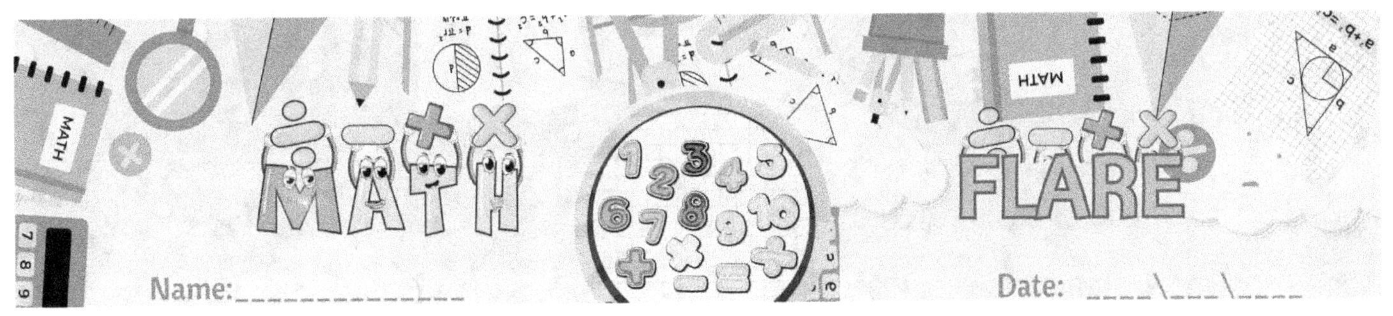

77. 89.17
   − 46.65

78. 1.9) 9.6

79. 1.9) 4.8

80. 51.94
   − 22.56

81. 45.52
   − 40.95

82. 62.19
   + 64.03

83. 8.4
   × 7.8

84. 47.64
   − 36.33

85. 4.2
   × 6.3

86. 5.9
   × 8.2

87. 96.48
   + 92.90

88. 41.84
   + 75.34

89. 84.69
   − 65.57

90. 75.13
   + 79.16

91. 9.6
   × 4.4

92. 4.2) 6.8

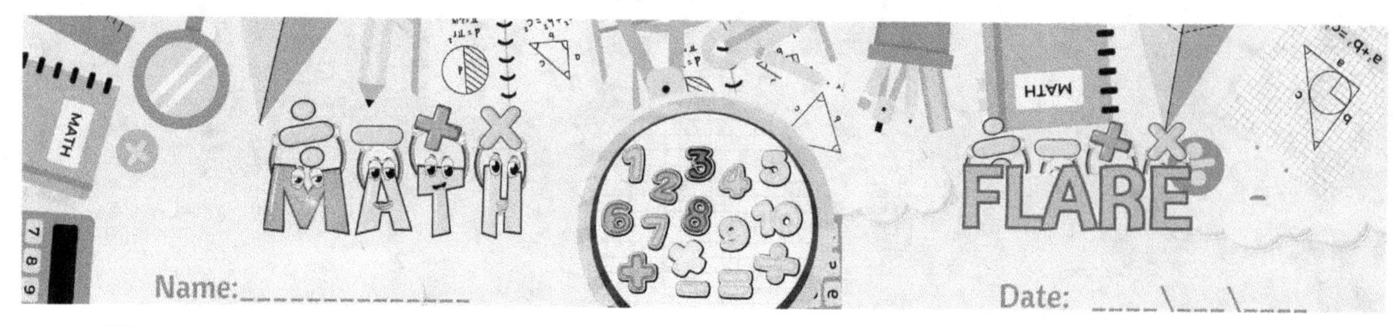

93. 5.3
   × 8.7

94. 5.4
   × 3.2

95. 4.9
   × 1.6

96. 71.55
   + 85.78

97. 6.1
   × 4.9

98. 6.5⟌6.7

99. 46.15
   − 15.88

100. 72.39
    − 13.54

101. 5.9
    × 6.1

102. 3.7
    × 2.7

103. 74.41
    − 35.95

104. 35.31
    + 51.93

105. 90.54
    + 54.97

106. 63.46
    − 40.26

107. 80.75
    − 43.39

108. 1.1⟌6.7

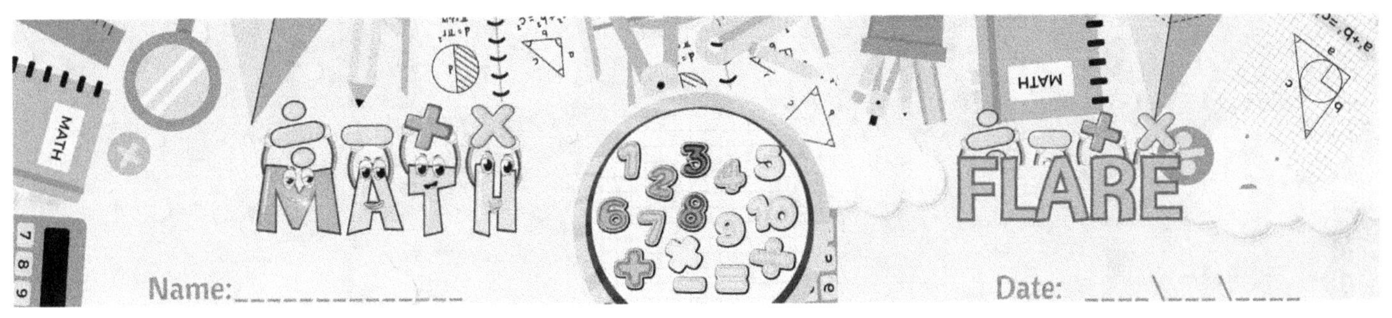

109.

$4.3\overline{)7.2}$

110.

$\begin{array}{r} 1.5 \\ \times\ 2.6 \\ \hline \end{array}$

111.

$6.8\overline{)8.7}$

112.

$6.9\overline{)8.8}$

113.

$\begin{array}{r} 9.5 \\ \times\ 7.9 \\ \hline \end{array}$

114.

$\begin{array}{r} 7.8 \\ \times\ 1.7 \\ \hline \end{array}$

115.

$\begin{array}{r} 94.44 \\ -\ 67.60 \\ \hline \end{array}$

116.

$\begin{array}{r} 55.67 \\ -\ 13.95 \\ \hline \end{array}$

117.

$\begin{array}{r} 91.32 \\ -\ 36.10 \\ \hline \end{array}$

118.

$1.7\overline{)7.3}$

119.

$8.8\overline{)9.0}$

120.

$\begin{array}{r} 65.93 \\ -\ 46.65 \\ \hline \end{array}$

121.

$\begin{array}{r} 99.84 \\ -\ 46.22 \\ \hline \end{array}$

122.

$1.9\overline{)2.0}$

123.

$\begin{array}{r} 84.04 \\ +\ 24.82 \\ \hline \end{array}$

124.

$1.1\overline{)9.2}$

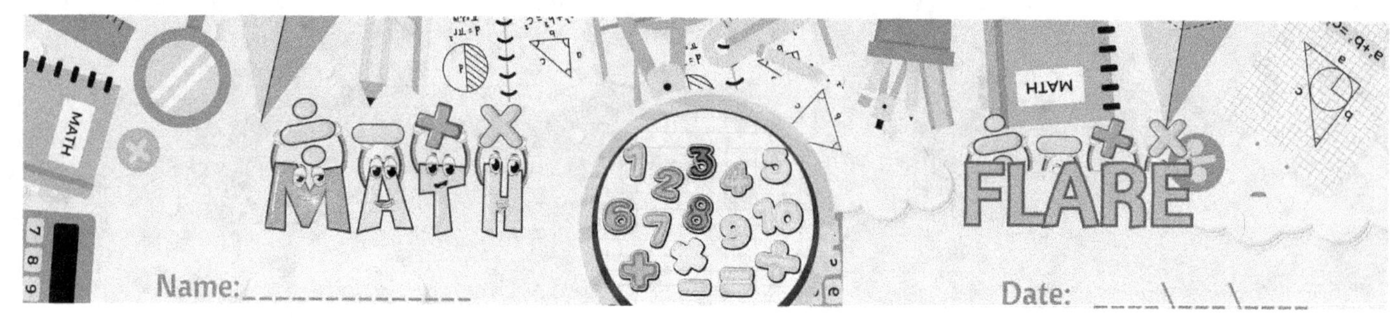

125. 57.93
    + 95.66

126. 92.82
    - 34.58

127. 90.26
    - 78.60

128. 38.95
    - 22.00

129. 55.01
    - 24.29

130. 3.6) 4.2

131. 74.26
    - 21.27

132. 24.09
    + 83.50

133. 3.2) 1.8

134. 5.0
    × 7.0

135. 7.6) 9.7

136. 8.6
    × 2.7

137. 13.22
    + 43.92

138. 5.3
    × 7.2

139. 75.94
    + 40.24

140. 8.9
    × 3.6

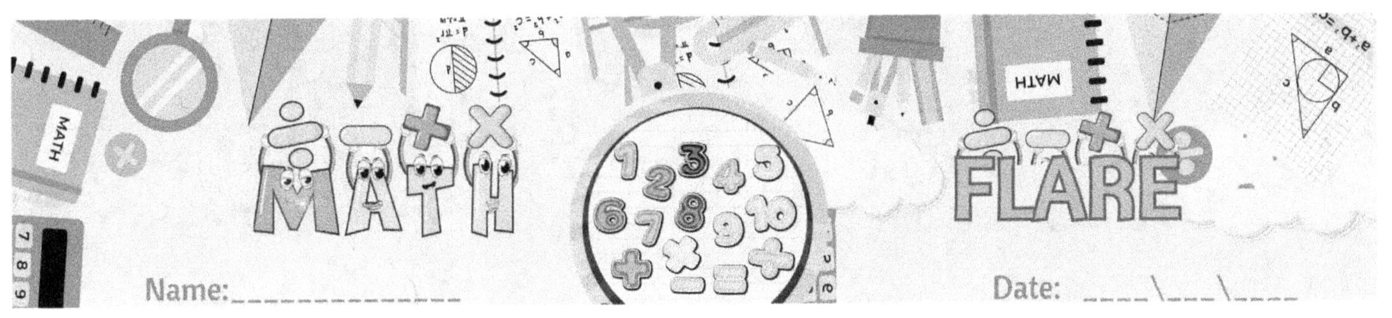

141. 7.6
    × 7.2

142. 6.7
    × 7.7

143. 28.47
    + 62.79

144. 28.07
    + 97.72

145. 2.2
    × 4.8

146. 7.8 ⟌ 8.9

147. 85.39
    − 78.53

148. 1.1 ⟌ 8.2

149. 7.0 ⟌ 6.4

150. 8.0 ⟌ 7.4

151. 88.91
    + 51.23

152. 87.40
    − 16.25

153. 64.84
    + 99.86

154. 62.74
    − 53.11

155. 55.57
    − 24.78

156. 86.39
    − 28.08

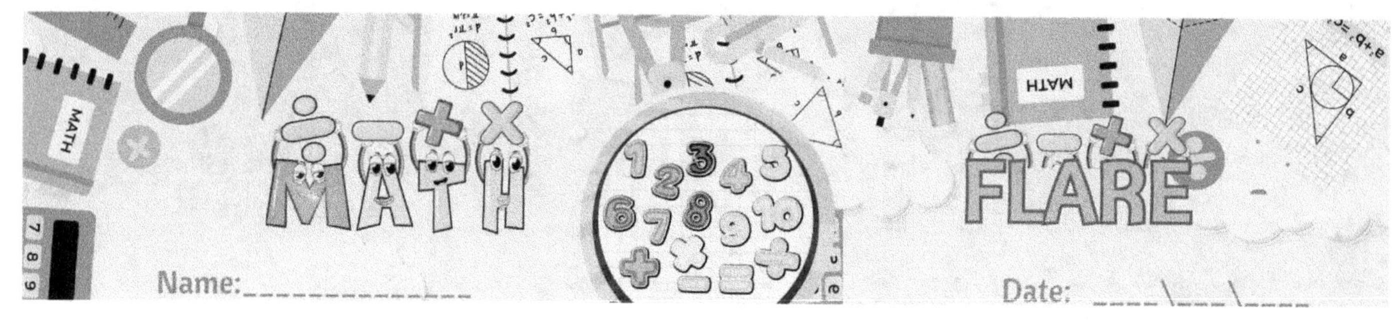

157. 2.8⟌1.9

158. 3.1
    × 5.4

159. 42.92
    + 72.91

160. 24.28
    + 65.58

161. 82.00
    − 18.46

162. 84.74
    + 89.85

163. 4.5
    × 8.2

164. 9.0
    × 1.1

165. 6.1⟌8.5

166. 11.44
    + 85.14

167. 40.86
    + 42.63

168. 64.28
    + 92.02

169. 4.2⟌8.0

170. 5.6
    × 9.6

171. 5.3
    × 4.9

172. 87.77
    − 58.82

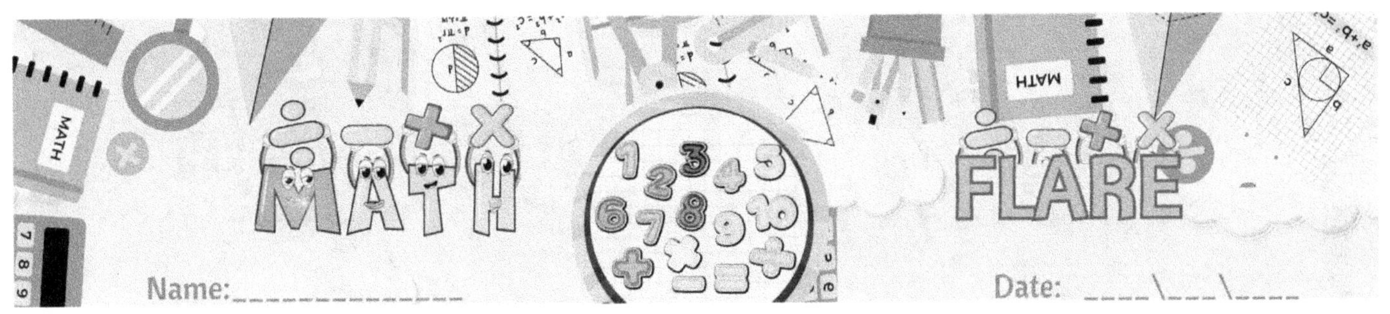

173.

$$1.6\overline{)7.0}$$

174.

$$\begin{array}{r} 57.93 \\ +\ 22.49 \\ \hline \end{array}$$

175.

$$\begin{array}{r} 70.27 \\ +\ 17.61 \\ \hline \end{array}$$

176.

$$4.7\overline{)2.8}$$

177.

$$\begin{array}{r} 43.13 \\ -\ 39.86 \\ \hline \end{array}$$

178.

$$\begin{array}{r} 91.81 \\ -\ 75.72 \\ \hline \end{array}$$

179.

$$3.0\overline{)2.9}$$

180.

$$\begin{array}{r} 8.2 \\ \times\ 2.1 \\ \hline \end{array}$$

181.

$$8.5\overline{)4.1}$$

182.

$$\begin{array}{r} 3.3 \\ \times\ 8.3 \\ \hline \end{array}$$

183.

$$2.8\overline{)7.8}$$

184.

$$\begin{array}{r} 48.61 \\ +\ 46.17 \\ \hline \end{array}$$

185.

$$\begin{array}{r} 96.60 \\ -\ 71.51 \\ \hline \end{array}$$

186.

$$8.6\overline{)8.3}$$

187.

$$\begin{array}{r} 3.0 \\ \times\ 6.8 \\ \hline \end{array}$$

188.

$$\begin{array}{r} 66.26 \\ -\ 63.15 \\ \hline \end{array}$$

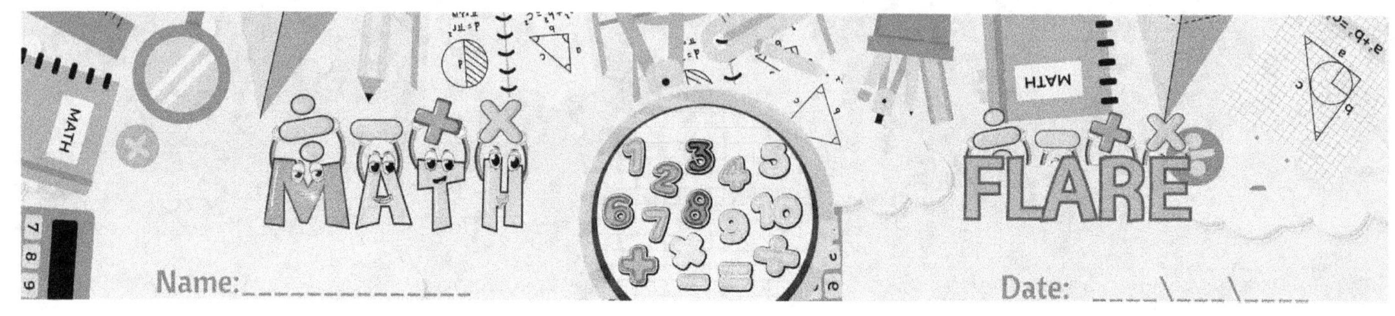

189.

$$4.2 \overline{)7.6}$$

190.

$$4.5 \overline{)3.4}$$

191.

$$9.0 \overline{)6.6}$$

192.

$$\begin{array}{r} 91.48 \\ +\ 12.43 \\ \hline \end{array}$$

193.

$$\begin{array}{r} 20.34 \\ -\ 13.95 \\ \hline \end{array}$$

194.

$$\begin{array}{r} 8.2 \\ \times\ 6.2 \\ \hline \end{array}$$

195.

$$\begin{array}{r} 8.4 \\ \times\ 5.2 \\ \hline \end{array}$$

196.

$$9.2 \overline{)2.1}$$

197.

$$\begin{array}{r} 34.47 \\ +\ 11.43 \\ \hline \end{array}$$

198.

$$\begin{array}{r} 44.45 \\ +\ 29.26 \\ \hline \end{array}$$

199.

$$\begin{array}{r} 24.74 \\ -\ 11.94 \\ \hline \end{array}$$

200.

$$\begin{array}{r} 67.76 \\ -\ 13.64 \\ \hline \end{array}$$

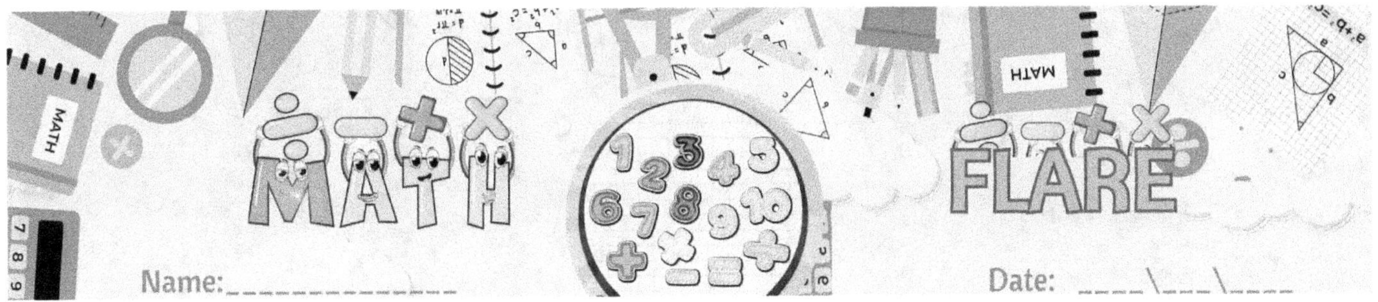

Exponents

Convert the values.

1. $12^{-3} =$ ___________________

2. $4^2 =$ ___________________

3. $19^{-2} =$ ___________________

4. $11^3 =$ ___________________

5. $17^{-3} =$ ___________________

6. $16^{-2} =$ ___________________

7. $12^2 =$ ___________________

8. $3^3 =$ ___________________

9. $16^{-3} =$ ___________________

10. $7^2 =$ ___________________

11. $2^2 =$ ___________________

12. $2^3 =$ ___________________

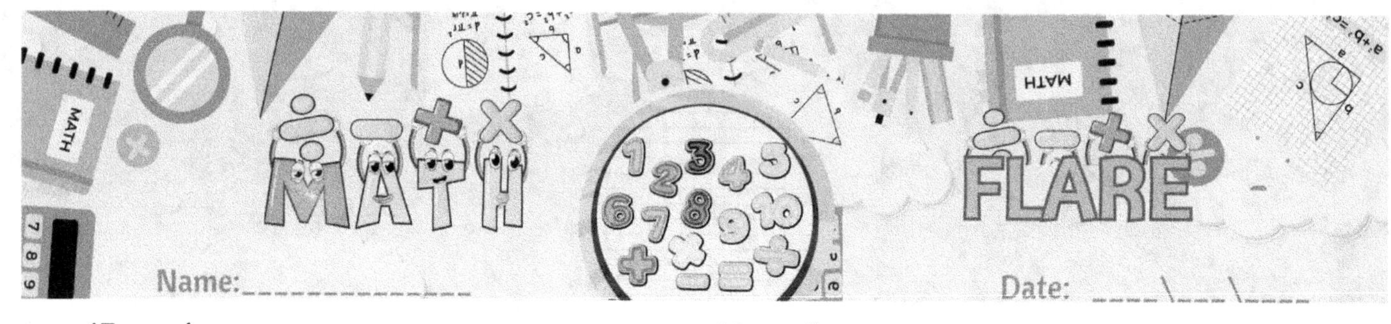

13. $5^4 =$ _______________

14. $5^3 =$ _______________

15. $1^{-3} =$ _______________

16. $10^{-2} =$ _______________

17. $20^2 =$ _______________

18. $9^{-3} =$ _______________

19. $16^2 =$ _______________

20. $15^{-2} =$ _______________

21. $8^4 =$ _______________

22. $11^4 =$ _______________

23. $3^4 =$ _______________

24. $3^{-3} =$ _______________

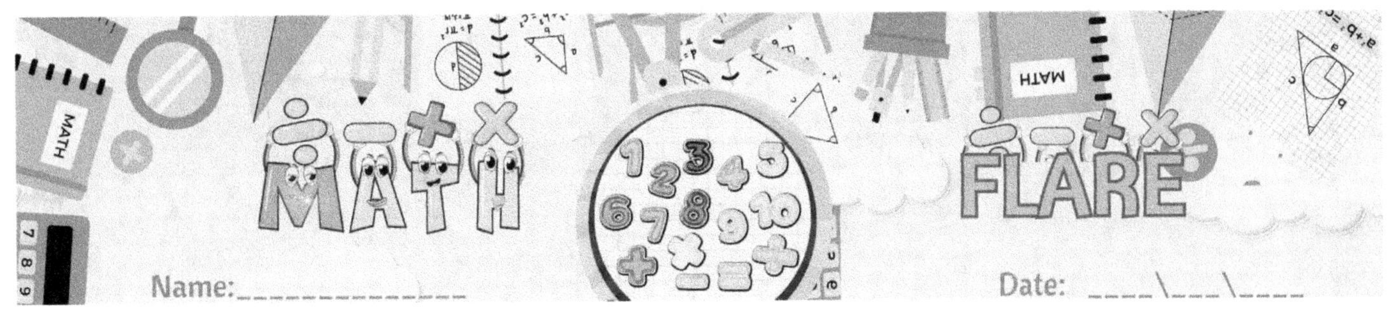

25. 1^3 = _______________

26. 2^{-3} = _______________

27. 17^{-2} = _______________

28. 20^3 = _______________

29. 6^3 = _______________

30. 12^{-2} = _______________

31. 8^{-3} = _______________

32. 15^{-3} = _______________

33. 2^4 = _______________

34. 7^{-2} = _______________

35. 18^2 = _______________

36. 8^2 = _______________

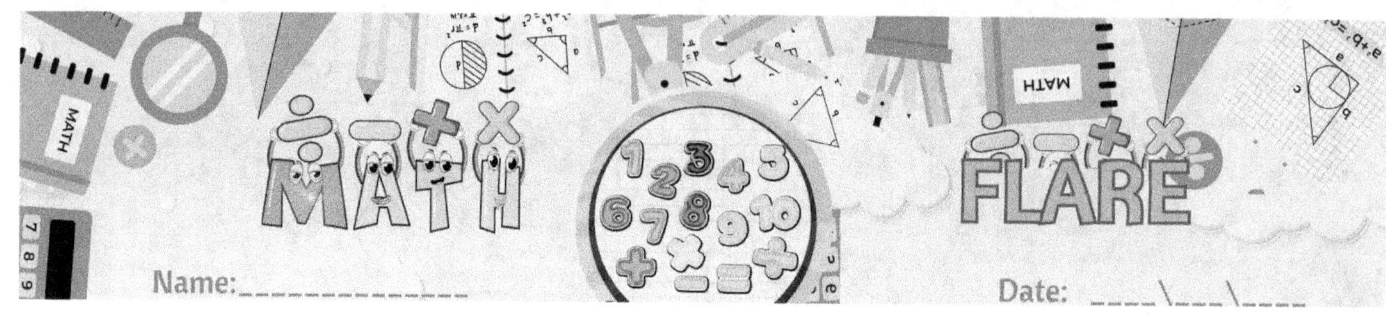

37. $17^2 =$ _______________

38. $13^{-3} =$ _______________

39. $6^4 =$ _______________

40. $12^4 =$ _______________

41. $8^{-2} =$ _______________

42. $5^2 =$ _______________

43. $3^{-2} =$ _______________

44. $7^4 =$ _______________

45. $6^2 =$ _______________

46. $1^{-2} =$ _______________

47. $4^{-3} =$ _______________

48. $4^3 =$ _______________

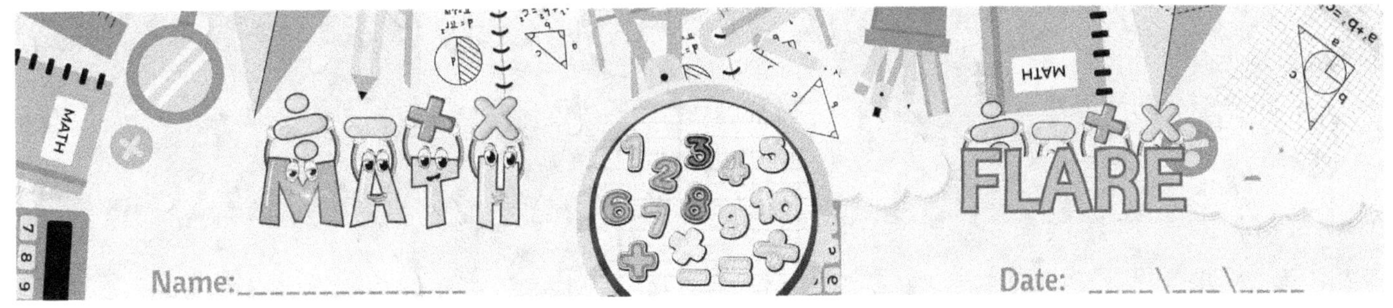

Name:___________________   Date: _____________

49. $1^4 =$

____

50. $19^2 =$

____

51. $15^4 =$

____

52. $11^{-2} =$

____

53. $14^{-2} =$

____

54. $18^{-3} =$

____

55. $4^4 =$

____

56. $13^4 =$

____

57. $11^{-3} =$

____

58. $16^3 =$

____

59. $17^3 =$

____

60. $16^4 =$

____

MathFlare - Pre-Algebra 4th to 6th Grade

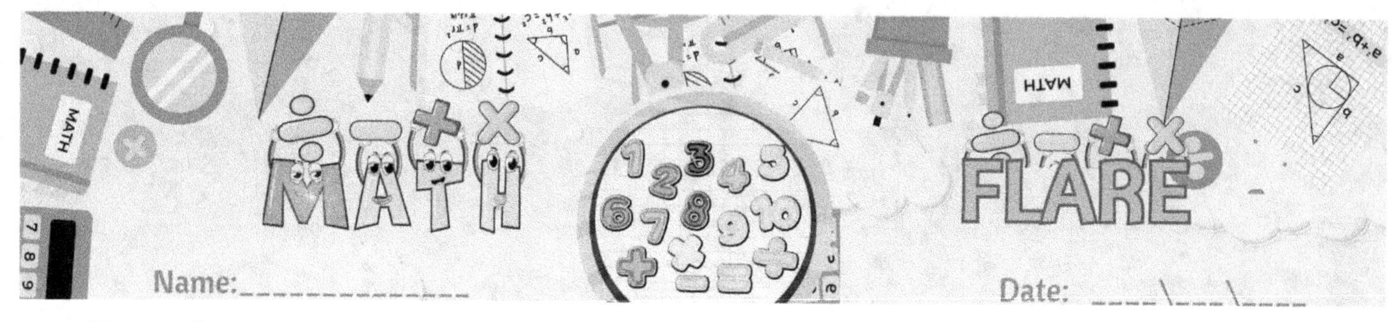

61. $14^2 =$ ___________________

62. $14^{-3} =$ ___________________

63. $13^3 =$ ___________________

64. $15^3 =$ ___________________

65. $11^2 =$ ___________________

66. $15^2 =$ ___________________

67. $17^4 =$ ___________________

68. $19^3 =$ ___________________

69. $12^3 =$ ___________________

70. $18^4 =$ ___________________

71. $19^4 =$ ___________________

72. $3^2 =$ ___________________

Square and Cube Roots

Calculate the root of each value.

1. $\sqrt{7{,}056} = $ _____________

2. $\sqrt[3]{1} = $ _____________

3. $\sqrt{1} = $ _____________

4. $\sqrt{100} = $ _____________

5. $\sqrt[4]{2{,}401} = $ _____________

6. $\sqrt[3]{8} = $ _____________

7. $\sqrt{4} = $ _____________

8. $\sqrt[3]{5{,}832} = $ _____________

9. $\sqrt[4]{10{,}000} = $ _____________

10. $\sqrt[4]{1{,}296} = $ _____________

11. $\sqrt{961} = $ _____________

12. $\sqrt[4]{16} = $ _____________

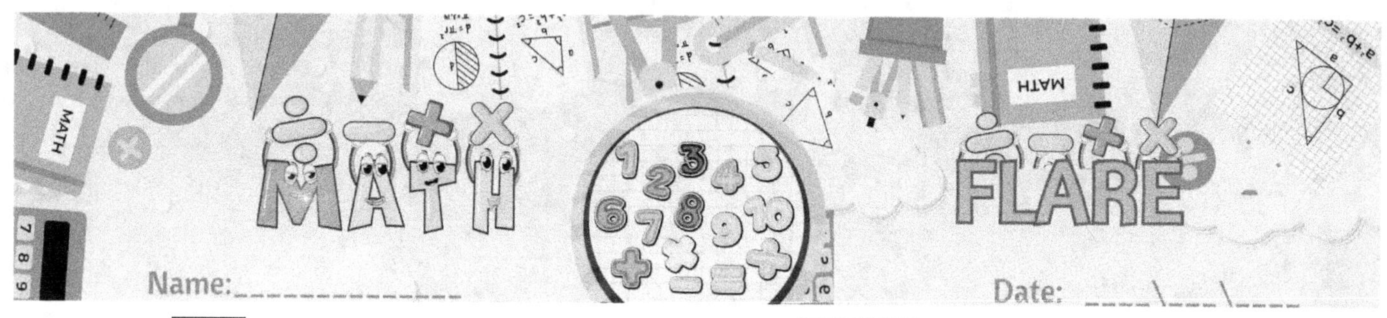

13. $\sqrt[3]{125}$ = _______________

14. $\sqrt[3]{1,000}$ = _______________

15. $\sqrt{81}$ = _______________

16. $\sqrt[4]{6,561}$ = _______________

17. $\sqrt[3]{343}$ = _______________

18. $\sqrt{36}$ = _______________

19. $\sqrt{3,721}$ = _______________

20. $\sqrt{324}$ = _______________

21. $\sqrt{676}$ = _______________

22. $\sqrt[3]{64}$ = _______________

23. $\sqrt{64}$ = _______________

24. $\sqrt[4]{81}$ = _______________

25. $\sqrt[4]{256}$ = _______________

26. $\sqrt{4,489}$ = _______________

27. $\sqrt{225}$ = _______________

28. $\sqrt{4{,}761}$ = _______________

29. $\sqrt[3]{4{,}913}$ = _______________

30. $\sqrt[4]{1}$ = _______________

31. $\sqrt[3]{1{,}728}$ = _______________

32. $\sqrt[4]{625}$ = _______________

33. $\sqrt{6{,}889}$ = _______________

34. $\sqrt{729}$ = _______________

35. $\sqrt[3]{27}$ = _______________

36. $\sqrt[3]{4{,}096}$ = _______________

37. $\sqrt[3]{9{,}261}$ = _______________

38. $\sqrt{8{,}281}$ = _______________

39. $\sqrt{3{,}364}$ = _______________

40. $\sqrt[3]{216}$ = _______________

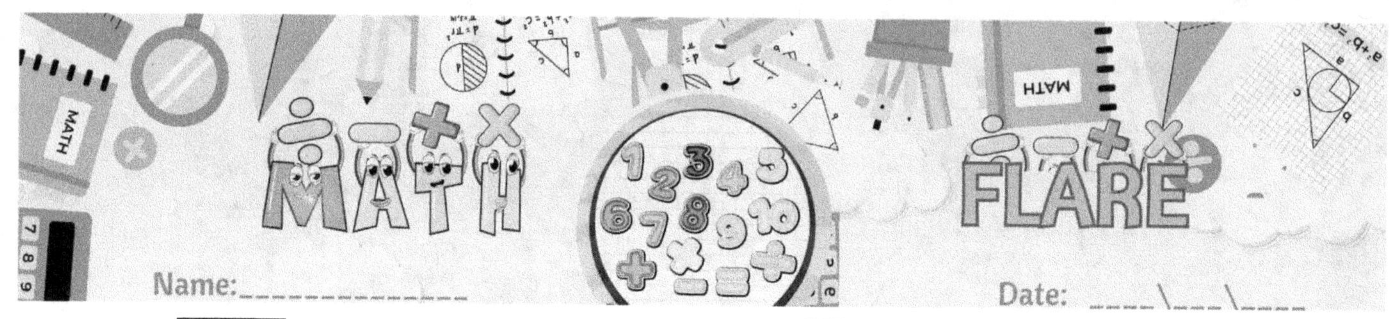

41. $\sqrt[3]{3,375}$ = _______________   42. $\sqrt{625}$ = _______________

43. $\sqrt{9}$ = _______________   44. $\sqrt[4]{4,096}$ = _______________

45. $\sqrt[3]{6,859}$ = _______________   46. $\sqrt{16}$ = _______________

47. $\sqrt{2,500}$ = _______________   48. $\sqrt{4,096}$ = _______________

49. $\sqrt{400}$ = _______________   50. $\sqrt[3]{10,648}$ = _______________

51. $\sqrt[3]{8,000}$ = _______________   52. $\sqrt{256}$ = _______________

53. $\sqrt{8,100}$ = _______________   54. $\sqrt{6,241}$ = _______________

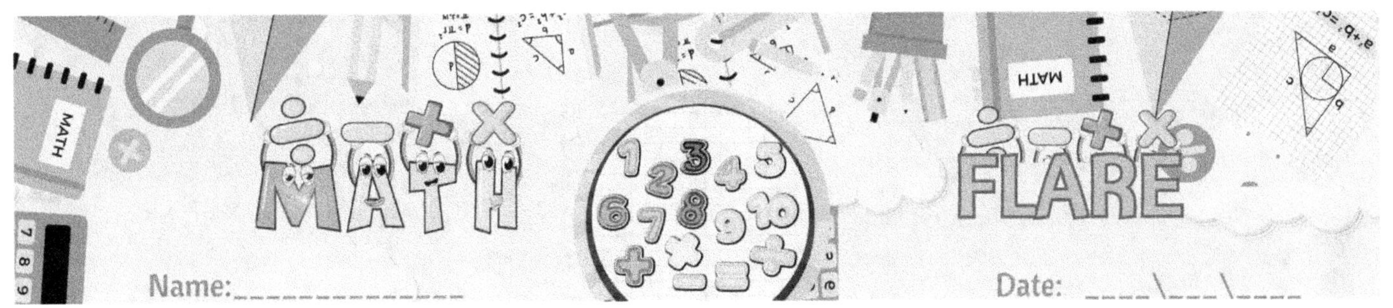

55. $\sqrt[3]{729}$ = _______________

56. $\sqrt{6,084}$ = _______________

57. $\sqrt{1,849}$ = _______________

58. $\sqrt[3]{1,331}$ = _______________

59. $\sqrt{484}$ = _______________

60. $\sqrt{49}$ = _______________

61. $\sqrt[3]{2,197}$ = _______________

62. $\sqrt{144}$ = _______________

63. $\sqrt{2,116}$ = _______________

64. $\sqrt{2,401}$ = _______________

65. $\sqrt[3]{512}$ = _______________

66. $\sqrt{529}$ = _______________

67. $\sqrt{1,444}$ = _______________

68. $\sqrt{8,464}$ = _______________

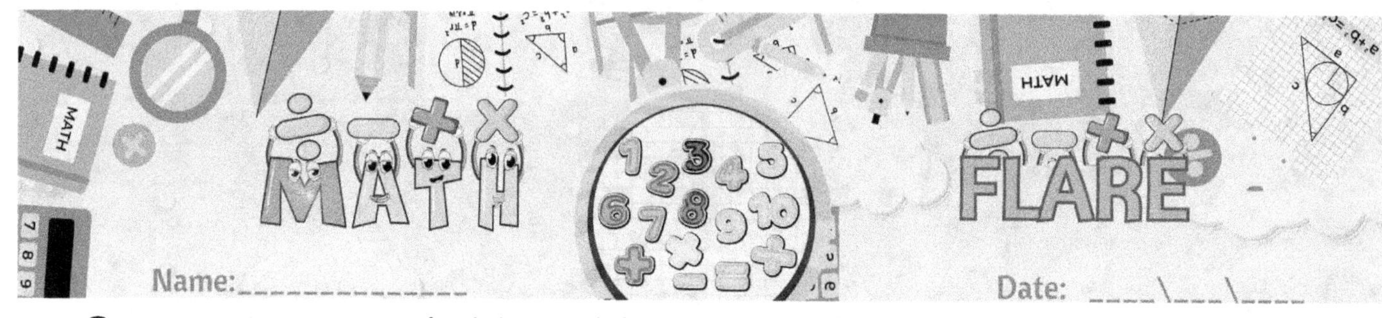

Operations with Mixed Numbers

Calculate.

1. $3\frac{3}{5} \div 4\frac{1}{4} =$ _______________________

2. $1\frac{3}{6} + 2\frac{1}{10} =$ _______________________

3. $9\frac{5}{8} - 6\frac{5}{7} =$ _______________________

4. $3\frac{1}{9} \times 4\frac{1}{2} =$ _______________________

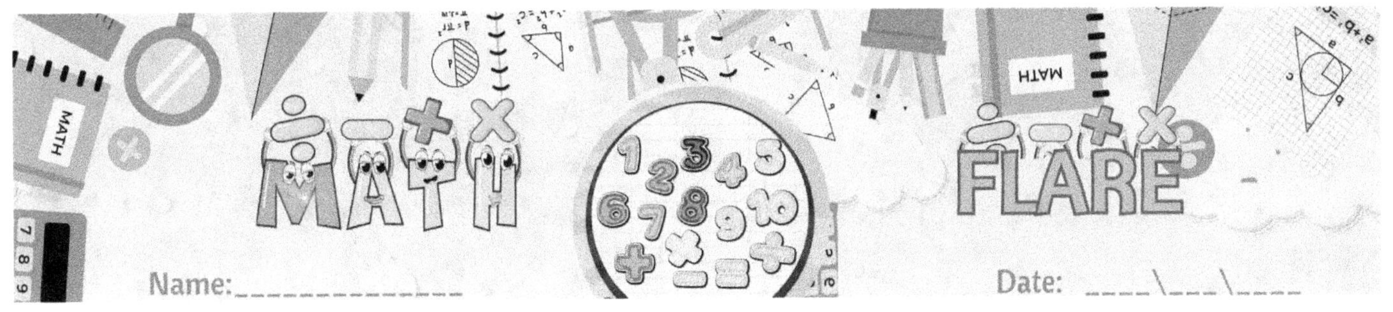

Name:____________________

Date: ____________

5. $9\frac{1}{3} - 6\frac{2}{4} =$ _______________________________

6. $5\frac{2}{5} + 1\frac{3}{6} =$ _______________________________

7. $3\frac{3}{5} \div 9\frac{5}{8} =$ _______________________________

8. $4\frac{2}{3} - 2\frac{2}{9} =$ _______________________________

9. $7\frac{1}{2} - 3\frac{8}{10} =$ _______________________________

10. $7\frac{6}{7} \times 3\frac{1}{4} =$ ________

11. $3\frac{1}{2} \div 7\frac{5}{6} =$ ________

12. $8\frac{1}{5} + 5\frac{1}{4} =$ ________

13. $6\frac{4}{10} \times 3\frac{3}{8} =$ ________

14. $5\frac{2}{3} \times 3\frac{2}{7} =$ ________

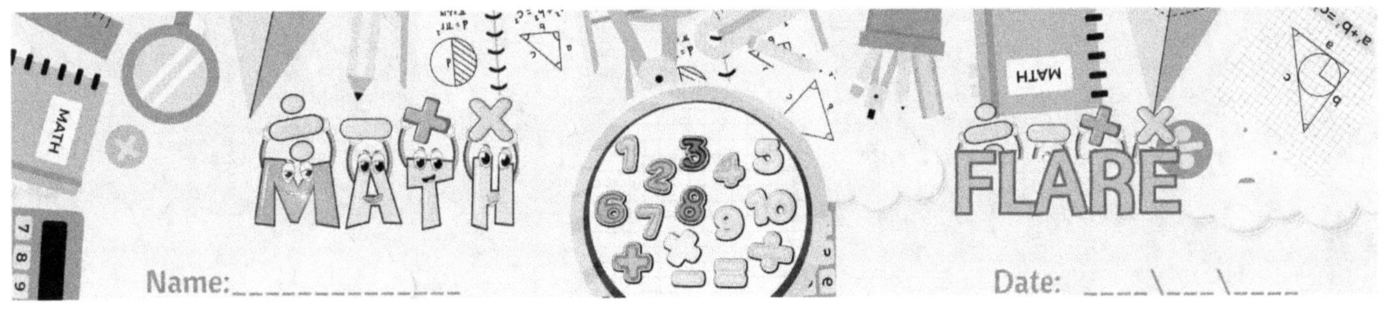

15. $1\frac{7}{9} + 1\frac{1}{5} =$ ___________________________

16. $4\frac{7}{9} + 8\frac{2}{4} =$ ___________________________

17. $5\frac{1}{2} + 4\frac{4}{6} =$ ___________________________

18. $3\frac{7}{10} + 2\frac{3}{8} =$ ___________________________

19. $1\frac{1}{3} \div 4\frac{6}{7} =$ ___________________________

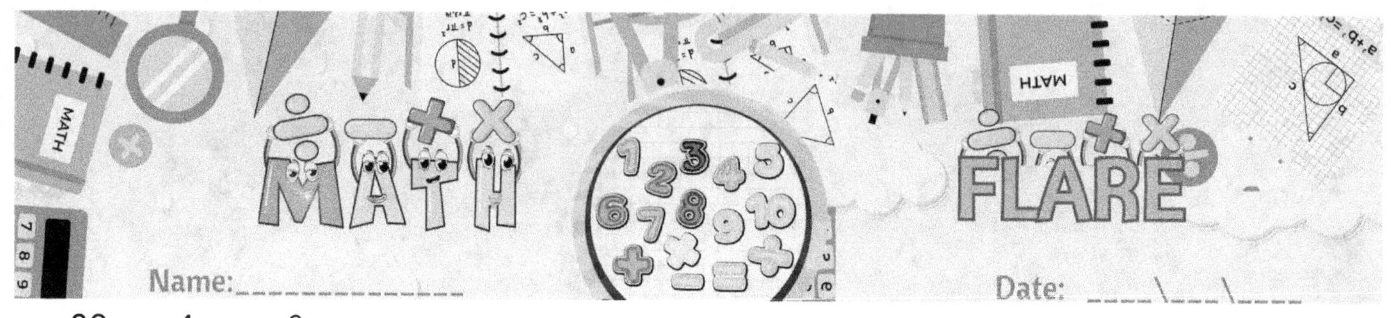

20. $4 \frac{4}{6} \times 3 \frac{2}{3} =$ ___________

21. $9 \frac{1}{8} + 6 \frac{6}{7} =$ ___________

22. $9 \frac{1}{5} - 8 \frac{1}{2} =$ ___________

23. $8 \frac{6}{10} \times 8 \frac{5}{9} =$ ___________

24. $8 \frac{2}{4} \times 6 \frac{8}{10} =$ ___________

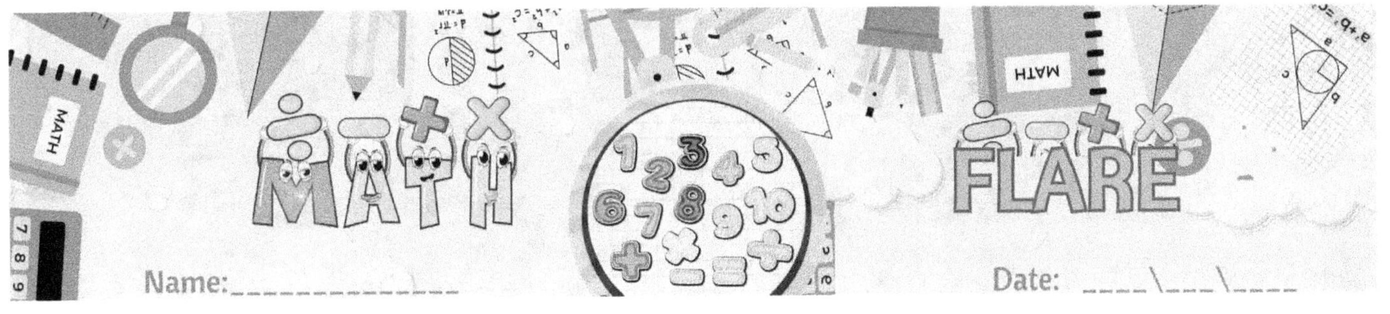

25. $3\frac{2}{5} + 5\frac{1}{2} = $ _______________________________

26. $8\frac{4}{9} - 4\frac{4}{8} = $ _______________________________

27. $8\frac{1}{4} - 8\frac{1}{7} = $ _______________________________

28. $8\frac{3}{6} + 7\frac{2}{3} = $ _______________________________

29. $1\frac{6}{7} \div 8\frac{3}{4} = $ _______________________________

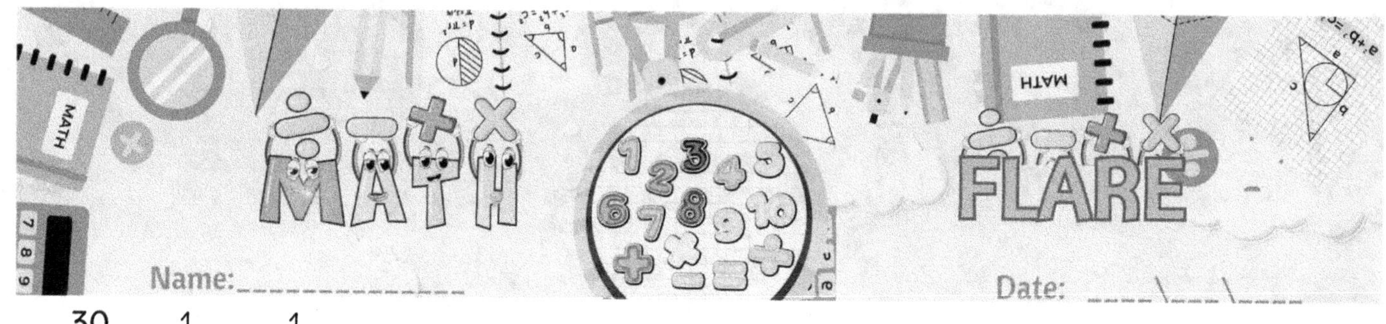

30. $4\frac{1}{2} \times 3\frac{1}{3} =$ _______________

31. $8\frac{3}{5} - 8\frac{1}{8} =$ _______________

32. $1\frac{1}{4} + 8\frac{2}{3} =$ _______________

33. $5\frac{5}{9} \div 8\frac{3}{7} =$ _______________

34. $7\frac{3}{5} - 1\frac{9}{10} =$ _______________

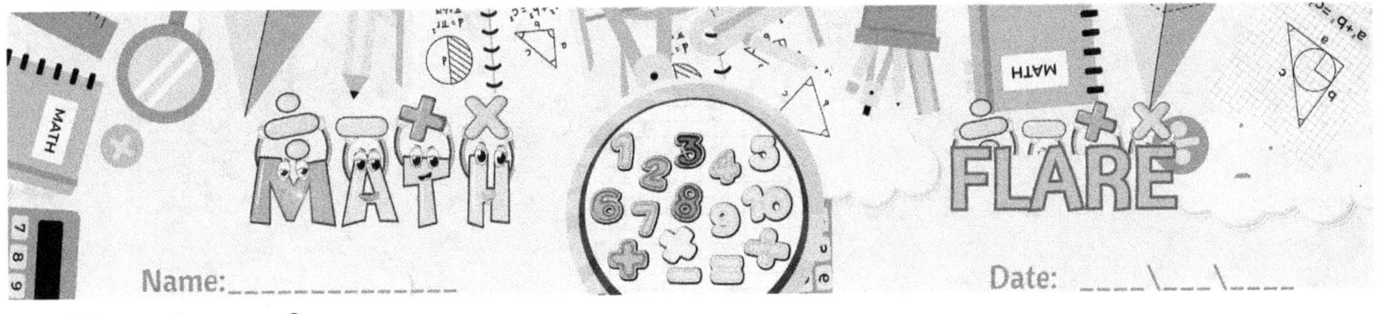

35. $5\frac{4}{5} - 5\frac{2}{6} =$ _______________

36. $6\frac{4}{8} \times 9\frac{1}{3} =$ _______________

37. $2\frac{2}{9} + 5\frac{2}{7} =$ _______________

38. $3\frac{1}{8} \times 4\frac{7}{9} =$ _______________

39. $8\frac{1}{2} - 8\frac{4}{10} =$ _______________

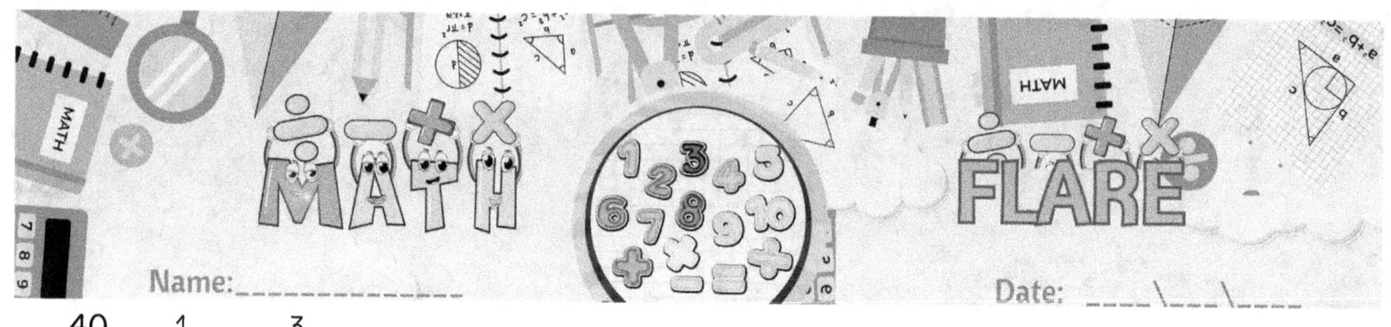

40. $7\frac{1}{6} - 3\frac{3}{7} =$ __________

41. $3\frac{1}{3} \times 4\frac{2}{3} =$ __________

42. $3\frac{4}{5} \times 4\frac{1}{2} =$ __________

43. $9\frac{6}{10} + 1\frac{5}{8} =$ __________

44. $6\frac{4}{7} + 1\frac{2}{4} =$ __________

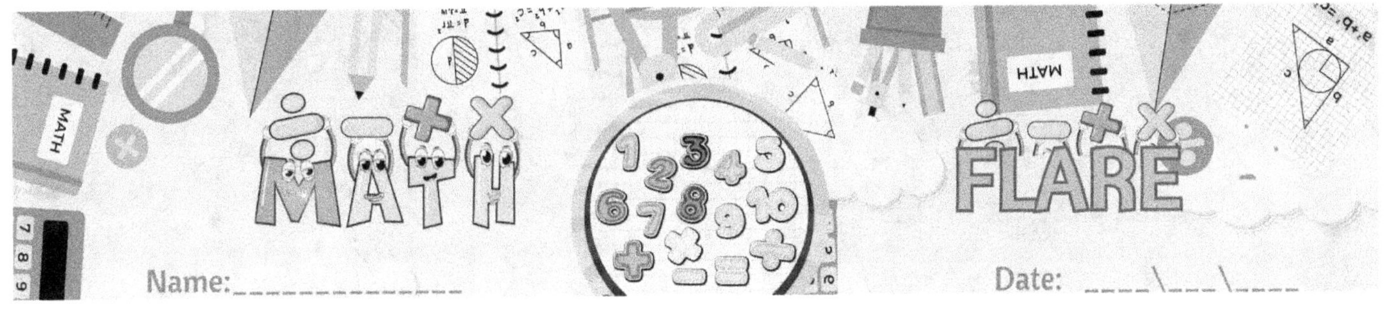

45. $9\frac{3}{6} - 8\frac{3}{9} = $ _______________

46. $7\frac{1}{2} - 5\frac{1}{4} = $ _______________

47. $3\frac{8}{9} - 2\frac{3}{10} = $ _______________

48. $8\frac{4}{7} - 5\frac{3}{5} = $ _______________

49. $6\frac{5}{6} + 2\frac{7}{8} = $ _______________

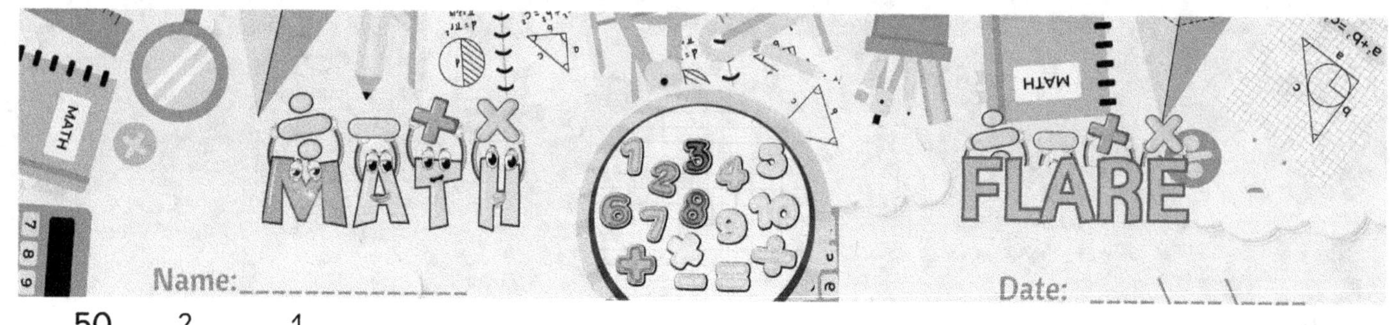

50. $7\frac{2}{3} + 8\frac{1}{2} =$ _______________________

51. $2\frac{6}{9} + 1\frac{2}{5} =$ _______________________

52. $4\frac{5}{10} + 8\frac{3}{8} =$ _______________________

53. $8\frac{2}{4} \div 4\frac{1}{6} =$ _______________________

54. $7\frac{2}{3} \div 8\frac{1}{7} =$ _______________________

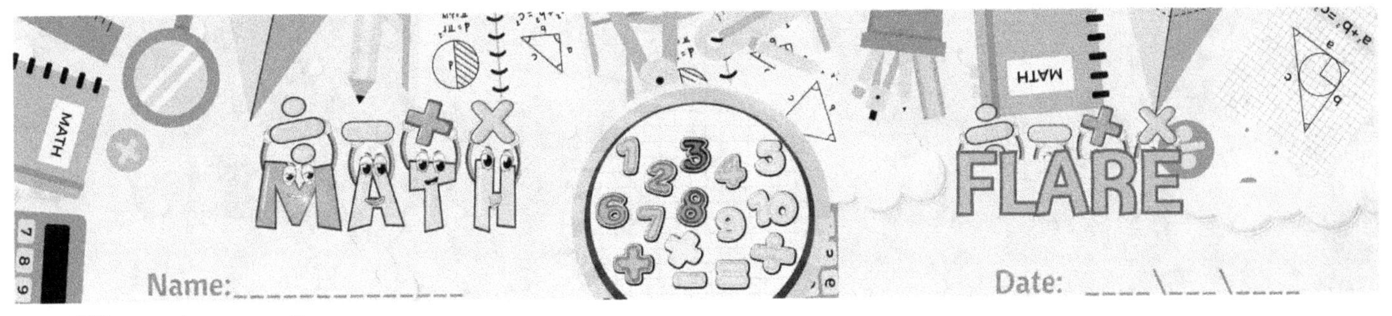

55. $9\frac{1}{6} - 8\frac{2}{9} =$ _______________

56. $9\frac{2}{5} \times 9\frac{3}{7} =$ _______________

57. $8\frac{2}{3} - 8\frac{2}{4} =$ _______________

58. $5\frac{1}{2} \times 2\frac{7}{10} =$ _______________

59. $8\frac{1}{2} - 8\frac{1}{4} =$ _______________

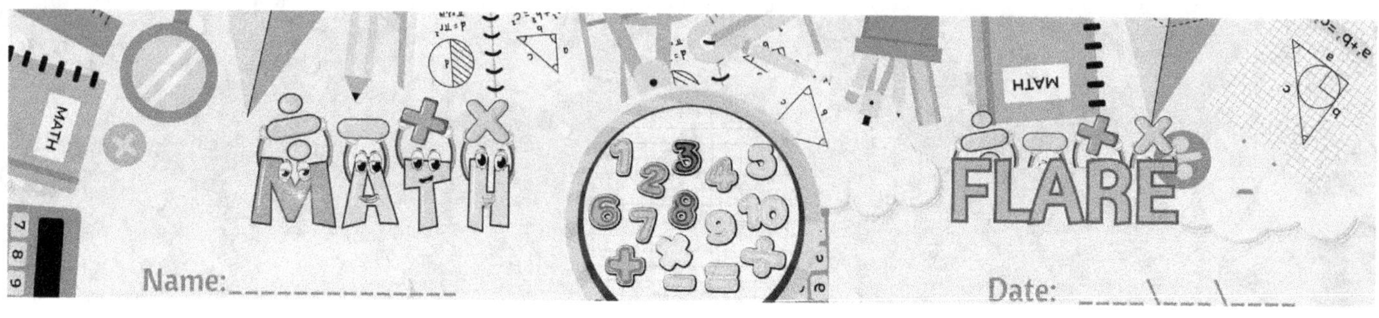

Multiple Operations with Fractions

Find the solution.

1. $\dfrac{4}{5} + \dfrac{3}{7} - \dfrac{1}{2} =$

2. $\dfrac{1}{3} + \dfrac{3}{8} - \dfrac{5}{8} =$

3. $\dfrac{1}{2} + \dfrac{1}{2} + \dfrac{2}{9} + \dfrac{2}{5} =$

4. $\dfrac{1}{4} + \dfrac{5}{9} + \dfrac{7}{8} =$

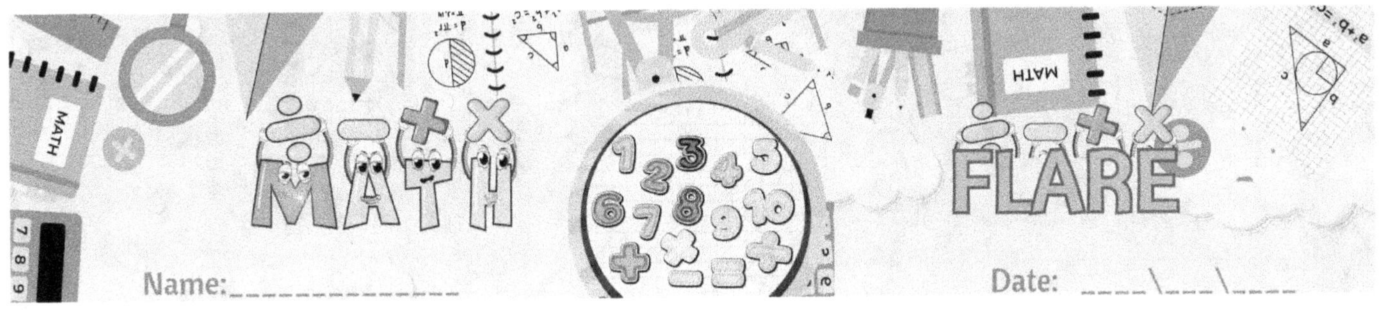

5. $\dfrac{1}{2} + \dfrac{1}{4} + \dfrac{1}{4} =$

6. $\dfrac{4}{5} + \dfrac{2}{9} - \dfrac{7}{10} =$

7. $\dfrac{1}{10} \times \dfrac{5}{9} \times \dfrac{1}{3} =$

8. $\dfrac{1}{10} + \dfrac{1}{4} - \dfrac{2}{3} =$

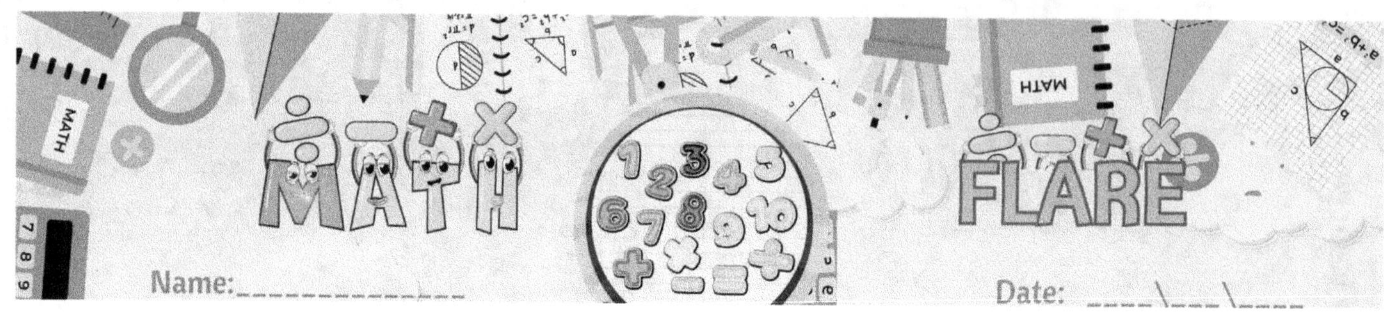

9. $\dfrac{1}{3} + \dfrac{3}{5} + \dfrac{4}{5} + \dfrac{3}{4} =$

10. $\dfrac{1}{2} \times \dfrac{4}{5} \times \dfrac{1}{4} =$

11. $\dfrac{5}{6} \times \dfrac{5}{8} \times \dfrac{5}{8} =$

12. $\dfrac{1}{5} + \dfrac{1}{7} + \dfrac{1}{4} =$

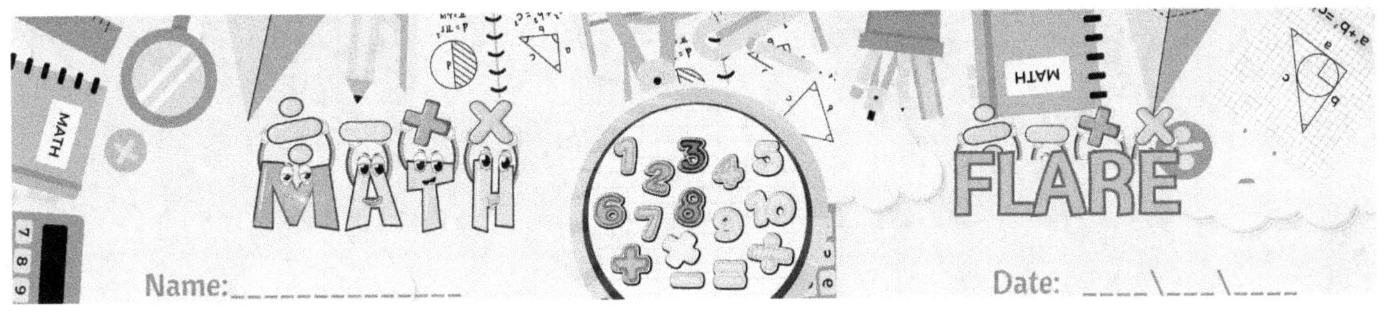

13. $\dfrac{4}{5} + \dfrac{3}{10} - \dfrac{5}{8} =$

14. $\dfrac{7}{10} + \dfrac{4}{5} - \dfrac{7}{10} =$

15. $\dfrac{1}{2} + \dfrac{1}{8} - \dfrac{5}{8} =$

16. $\dfrac{1}{6} + \dfrac{5}{8} + \dfrac{3}{4} + \dfrac{1}{6} =$

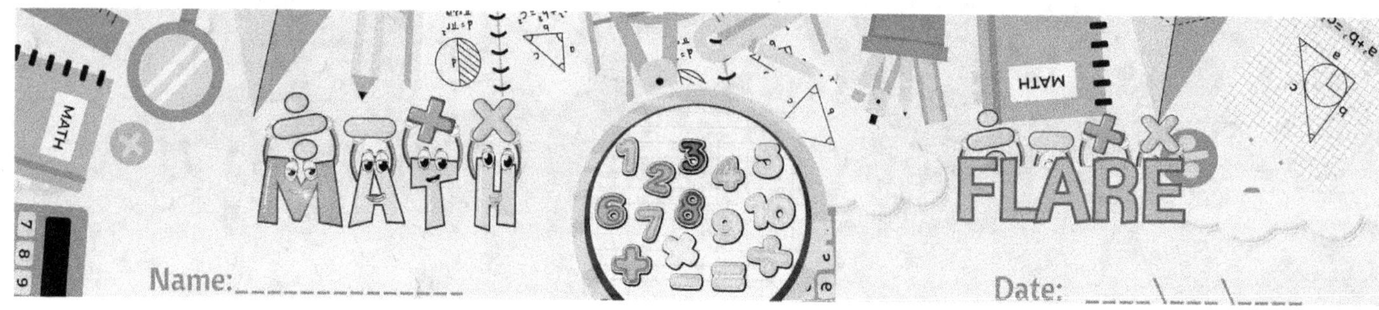

17. $\dfrac{1}{4} + \dfrac{1}{8} - \dfrac{3}{8} =$

18. $\dfrac{3}{4} + \dfrac{2}{3} + \dfrac{1}{6} + \dfrac{3}{10} =$

19. $\dfrac{1}{4} + \dfrac{1}{3} + \dfrac{1}{4} + \dfrac{7}{9} =$

20. $\dfrac{3}{8} + \dfrac{1}{2} + \dfrac{3}{8} + \dfrac{3}{4} =$

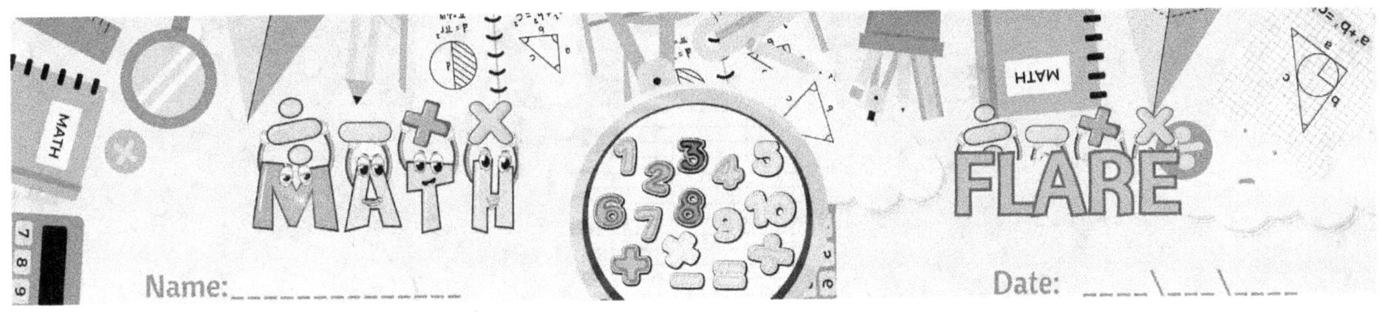

21. $\dfrac{1}{6} + \dfrac{4}{9} - \dfrac{2}{3} =$

22. $\dfrac{7}{8} + \dfrac{1}{6} - \dfrac{2}{3} =$

23. $\dfrac{1}{4} \times \dfrac{3}{8} \times \dfrac{4}{9} =$

24. $\dfrac{2}{3} + \dfrac{3}{10} + \dfrac{3}{10} + \dfrac{3}{8} =$

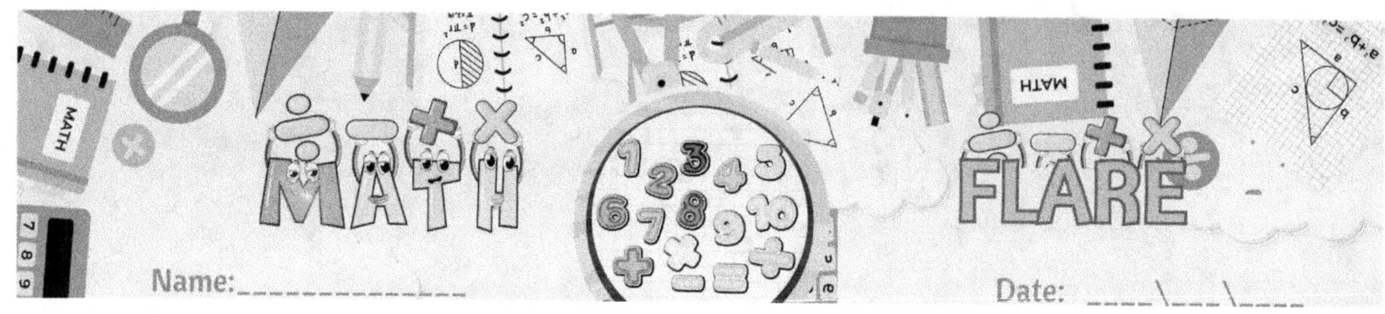

25. $\dfrac{5}{9} + \dfrac{3}{8} + \dfrac{1}{4} =$

26. $\dfrac{7}{8} + \dfrac{1}{7} + \dfrac{1}{2} + \dfrac{2}{5} =$

27. $\dfrac{1}{10} + \dfrac{1}{4} + \dfrac{8}{9} + \dfrac{1}{7} =$

28. $\dfrac{5}{8} \times \dfrac{5}{9} \times \dfrac{2}{3} =$

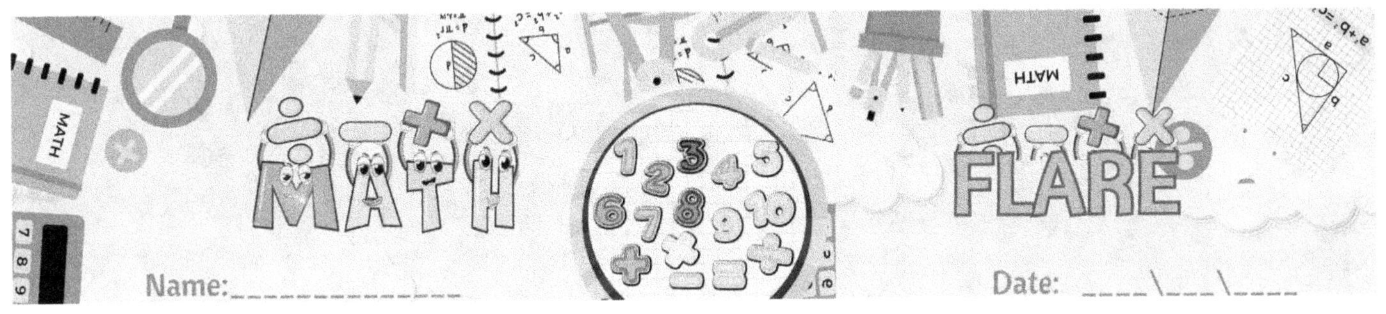

29. $\dfrac{2}{3} + \dfrac{1}{6} - \dfrac{7}{10} =$

30. $\dfrac{1}{3} + \dfrac{1}{3} + \dfrac{1}{4} + \dfrac{1}{3} =$

31. $\dfrac{1}{6} + \dfrac{1}{2} - \dfrac{2}{3} =$

32. $\dfrac{4}{5} + \dfrac{5}{8} + \dfrac{9}{10} =$

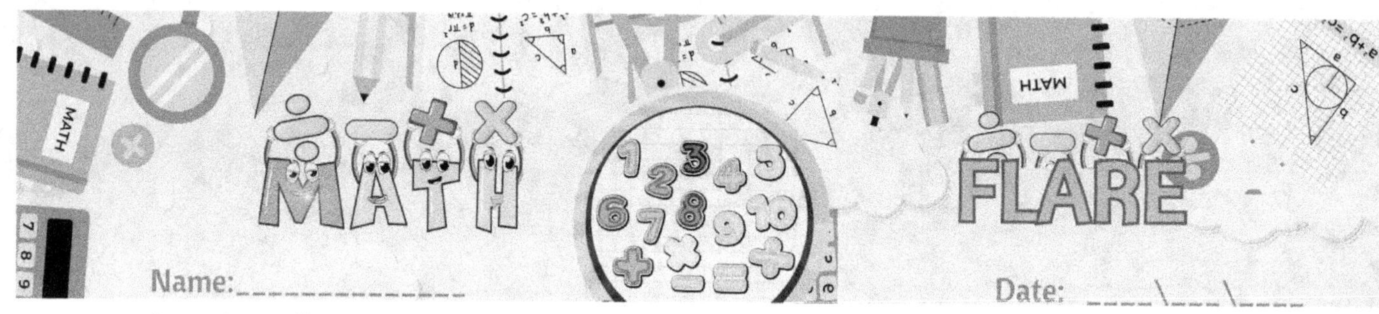

33. $\dfrac{1}{8} \times \dfrac{1}{6} \times \dfrac{9}{10} =$

34. $\dfrac{1}{2} \times \dfrac{1}{3} \times \dfrac{5}{6} =$

35. $\dfrac{3}{10} + \dfrac{1}{2} - \dfrac{2}{3} =$

36. $\dfrac{1}{4} + \dfrac{6}{7} + \dfrac{3}{10} + \dfrac{1}{2} =$

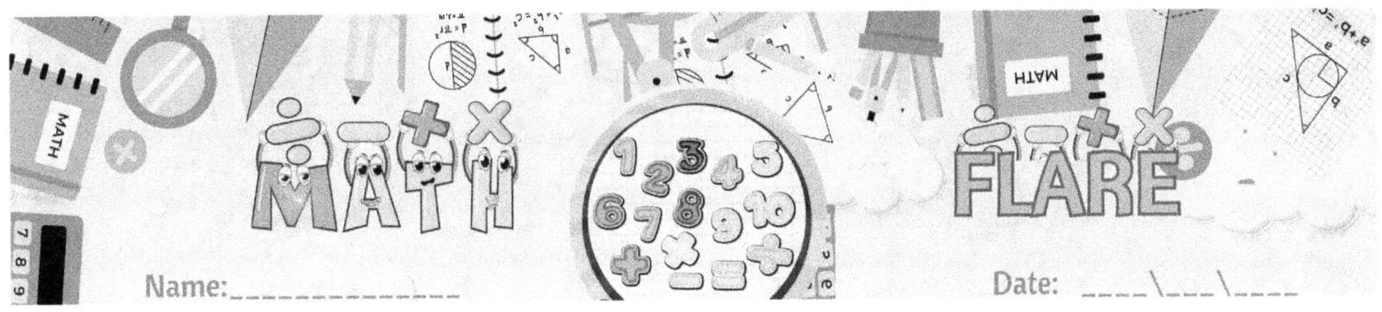

37. $\dfrac{1}{8} + \dfrac{1}{6} - \dfrac{1}{8} =$

38. $\dfrac{1}{2} + \dfrac{1}{2} + \dfrac{1}{3} =$

39. $\dfrac{1}{4} + \dfrac{6}{7} + \dfrac{1}{4} + \dfrac{1}{5} =$

40. $\dfrac{4}{5} + \dfrac{1}{2} + \dfrac{5}{6} + \dfrac{1}{8} =$

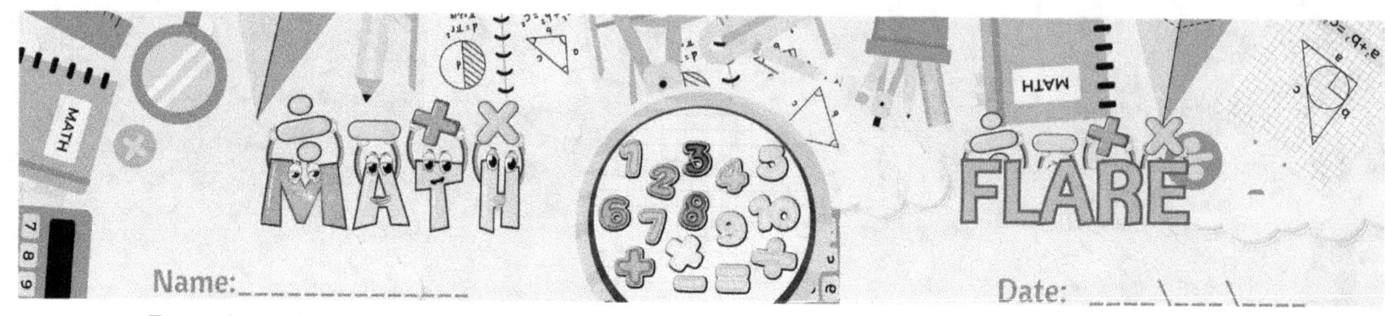

41. $\dfrac{5}{7} + \dfrac{1}{2} + \dfrac{2}{9} =$

42. $\dfrac{1}{7} + \dfrac{1}{5} + \dfrac{1}{6} + \dfrac{1}{8} =$

43. $\dfrac{2}{5} + \dfrac{1}{6} + \dfrac{1}{2} + \dfrac{1}{4} =$

44. $\dfrac{5}{6} \times \dfrac{4}{5} \times \dfrac{2}{5} =$

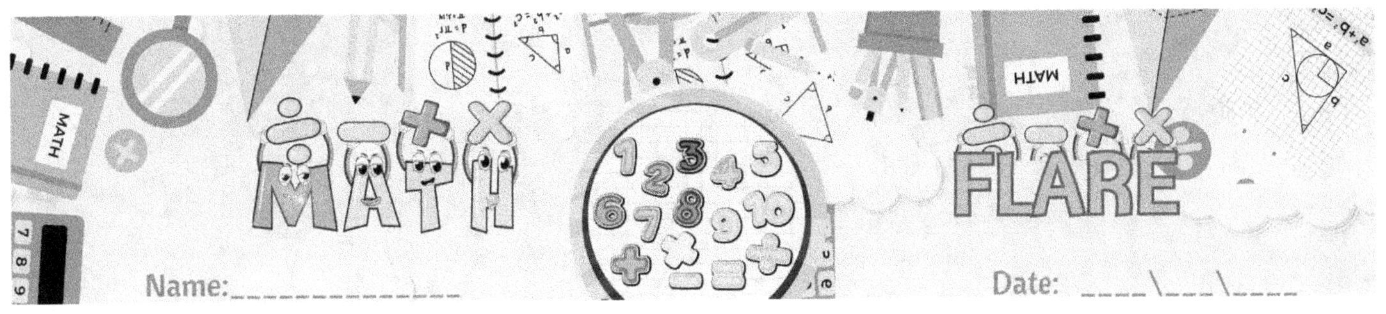

45. $\dfrac{1}{2} + \dfrac{1}{2} - \dfrac{1}{6} =$

46. $\dfrac{7}{10} + \dfrac{2}{3} + \dfrac{2}{3} =$

47. $\dfrac{1}{8} + \dfrac{5}{7} + \dfrac{1}{3} + \dfrac{1}{2} =$

48. $\dfrac{1}{6} + \dfrac{1}{6} + \dfrac{1}{8} =$

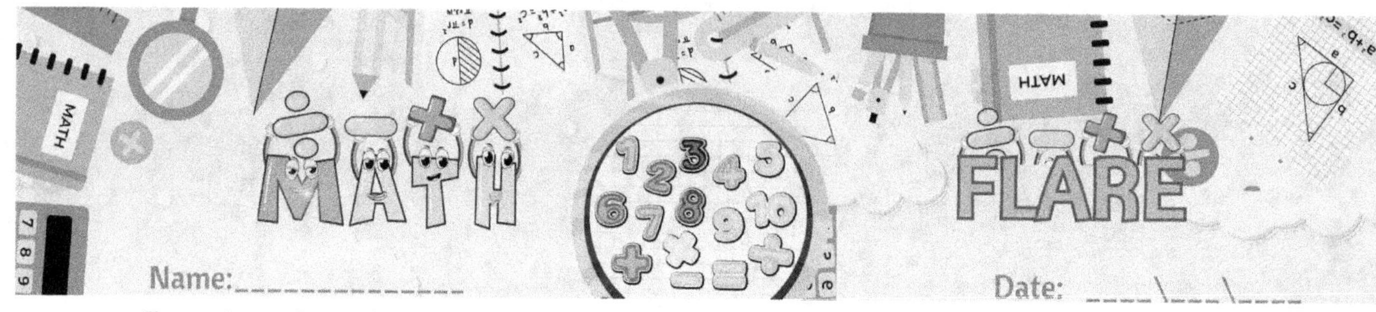

49. $\dfrac{5}{6} + \dfrac{1}{2} + \dfrac{1}{3} + \dfrac{1}{6} =$

50. $\dfrac{2}{9} + \dfrac{1}{3} + \dfrac{5}{6} =$

51. $\dfrac{1}{2} \times \dfrac{3}{10} \times \dfrac{5}{8} =$

52. $\dfrac{4}{7} + \dfrac{4}{5} + \dfrac{9}{10} + \dfrac{1}{8} =$

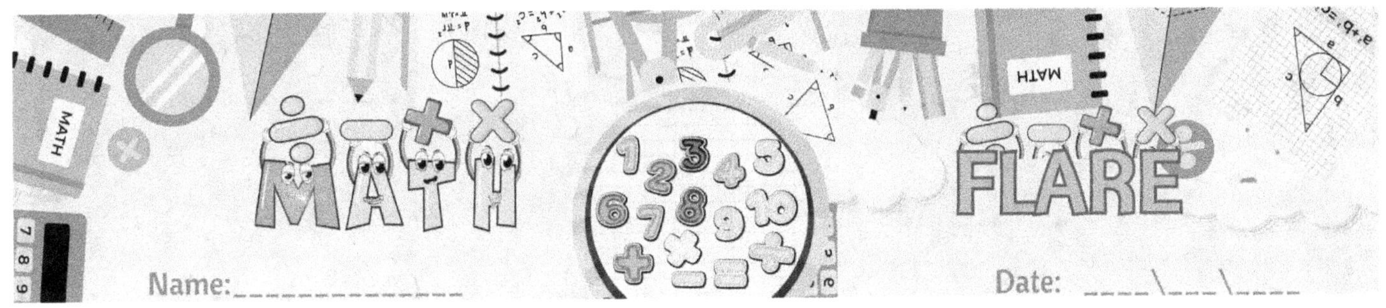

53. $\dfrac{1}{2} + \dfrac{4}{9} + \dfrac{2}{3} + \dfrac{1}{6} =$

54. $\dfrac{3}{5} + \dfrac{1}{2} - \dfrac{3}{8} =$

55. $\dfrac{1}{2} + \dfrac{3}{5} - \dfrac{3}{10} =$

56. $\dfrac{2}{3} \times \dfrac{2}{3} \times \dfrac{5}{6} =$

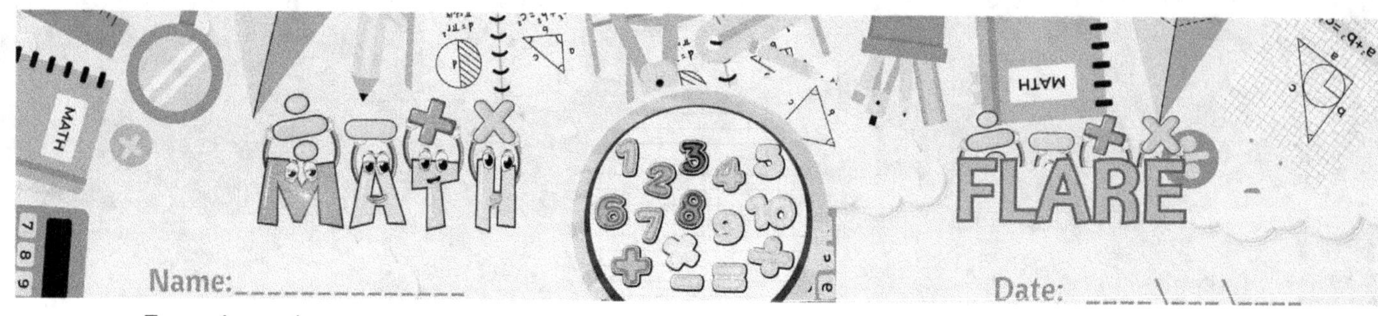

57. $\dfrac{5}{7} \times \dfrac{1}{6} \times \dfrac{1}{4} =$

58. $\dfrac{3}{8} \times \dfrac{1}{10} \times \dfrac{1}{2} =$

59. $\dfrac{3}{8} \times \dfrac{2}{7} \times \dfrac{6}{7} =$

60. $\dfrac{9}{10} \times \dfrac{3}{7} \times \dfrac{1}{9} =$

ANSWERS

Page 1: Operations with Whole Numbers

1. -13	2. -17	3. 3	4. 14	5. -2	6. -5	7. 3	8. 2
9. -12	10. -6	11. -8	12. -9	13. -5	14. -5	15. -1	16. 11
17. -6	18. 7	19. -8	20. 4	21. 3	22. -12	23. 3	24. -3
25. -7	26. 6	27. 5	28. 8	29. -2	30. 0	31. 1	32. -8
33. 4	34. 7	35. 0	36. 5	37. 10	38. 5	39. -8	40. -7
41. -1	42. 1	43. 4	44. 0	45. 14	46. -9	47. 15	48. 7
49. -13	50. 8	51. -12	52. -5	53. -14	54. 12	55. 1	56. -12
57. -12	58. 5	59. 10	60. 7	61. -4	62. 2	63. -7	64. -24
65. 6	66. -5	67. 3	68. -3	69. 5	70. 8	71. 6	72. 6
73. -11	74. -8	75. 10	76. -8	77. -13	78. 8	79. 6	80. 5
81. 8	82. 4	83. 6	84. 19	85. -7	86. 7	87. 8	88. -9
89. 7	90. -16	91. 8	92. -4	93. 11	94. 5	95. 8	96. -17
97. 4	98. 8						

Page 11: Operations with Decimals

1. 166.96	2. 45.00	3. 20.85	4. 18.81	5. 44.12
6. 135.76	7. 42.78	8. 1.1	9. 1.6	10. 9.24
11. 3.00	12. 111.55	13. 58.93	14. 0.5	15. 7.02
16. 55.50	17. 12.23	18. 56.27	19. 65.32	20. 1.8
21. 71.06	22. 112.55	23. 15.34	24. 0.5	25. 122.53

26. 30.03   27. 37.21   28. 6.37   29. 5.61   30. 103.42

31. 29.11   32. 1   33. 33.89   34. 48.99   35. 102.29

36. 8.43   37. 79.31   38. 8.40   39. 0.6   40. 1.6

41. 3.4   42. 151.61   43. 1.1   44. 74.31   45. 95.08

46. 1.2   47. 76.56   48. 110.85   49. 125.06   50. 76.49

51. 0.6   52. 37.60   53. 31.50   54. 1.0   55. 31.35

56. 57.63   57. 160.07   58. 2.10   59. 124.25   60. 45.77

61. 3.1   62. 0.9   63. 34.47   64. 5.9   65. 15.49

66. 1.3   67. 94.23   68. 36.96   69. 43.20   70. 0.2

71. 109.41   72. 144.68   73. 4.20   74. 38.72   75. 3.03

76. 130.62   77. 42.52   78. 5.1   79. 2.5   80. 29.38

81. 4.57   82. 126.22   83. 65.52   84. 11.31   85. 26.46

86. 48.38   87. 189.38   88. 117.18   89. 19.12   90. 154.29

91. 42.24   92. 1.6   93. 46.11   94. 17.28   95. 7.84

96. 157.33   97. 29.89   98. 1.0   99. 30.27   100. 58.85

101. 35.99   102. 9.99   103. 38.46   104. 87.24   105. 145.51

106. 23.20   107. 37.36   108. 6.1   109. 1.7   110. 3.90

111. 1.3   112. 1.3   113. 75.05   114. 13.26   115. 26.84

116. 41.72   117. 55.22   118. 4.3   119. 1.0   120. 19.28

121. 53.62   122. 1.1   123. 108.86   124. 8.4   125. 153.59

126. 58.24   127. 11.66   128. 16.95   129. 30.72   130. 1.2

131. 52.99   132. 107.59   133. 0.6   134. 35.00   135. 1.3

136. 23.22   137. 57.14   138. 38.16   139. 116.18   140. 32.04

141. 54.72   142. 51.59   143. 91.26   144. 125.79   145. 10.56

146. 1.1   147. 6.86   148. 7.5   149. 0.9   150. 0.9

151. 140.14   152. 71.15   153. 164.70   154. 9.63   155. 30.79

156. 58.31   157. 0.7   158. 16.74   159. 115.83   160. 89.86

161. 63.54   162. 174.59   163. 36.90   164. 9.90   165. 1.4

166. 96.58   167. 83.49   168. 156.30   169. 1.9   170. 53.76

171. 25.97   172. 28.95   173. 4.4   174. 80.42   175. 87.88

176. 0.6   177. 3.27   178. 16.09   179. 1.0   180. 17.22

181. 0.5   182. 27.39   183. 2.8   184. 94.78   185. 25.09

186. 1.0   187. 20.40   188. 3.11   189. 1.8   190. 0.8

191. 0.7   192. 103.91   193. 6.39   194. 50.84   195. 43.68

196. 0.2   197. 45.90   198. 73.71   199. 12.80   200. 54.12

Page 24: Exponents

1. 1/1728   2. 16   3. 1/361   4. 1,331   5. 1/4913

6. 1/256   7. 144   8. 27   9. 1/4096   10. 49

11. 4   12. 8   13. 625   14. 125   15. 1

16. 1/100   17. 400   18. 1/729   19. 256   20. 1/225

21. 4,096   22. 14,641   23. 81   24. 1/27   25. 1

26. 1/8   27. 1/289   28. 8,000   29. 216   30. 1/144

31. 1/512 32. 1/3375 33. 16 34. 1/49 35. 324

36. 64 37. 289 38. 1/2197 39. 1,296 40. 20,736

41. 1/64 42. 25 43. 1/9 44. 2,401 45. 36

46. 1 47. 1/64 48. 64 49. 1 50. 361

51. 50,625 52. 1/121 53. 1/196 54. 1/5832 55. 256

56. 28,561 57. 1/1331 58. 4,096 59. 4,913 60. 65,536

61. 196 62. 1/2744 63. 2,197 64. 3,375 65. 121

66. 225 67. 83,521 68. 6,859 69. 1,728 70. 104,976

71. 130,321 72. 9

Page 30: Square and Cube Roots

1. 84 2. 1 3. 1 4. 10 5. 7 6. 2 7. 2 8. 18

9. 10 10. 6 11. 31 12. 2 13. 5 14. 10 15. 9 16. 9

17. 7 18. 6 19. 61 20. 18 21. 26 22. 4 23. 8 24. 3

25. 4 26. 67 27. 15 28. 69 29. 17 30. 1 31. 12 32. 5

33. 83 34. 27 35. 3 36. 16 37. 21 38. 91 39. 58 40. 6

41. 15 42. 25 43. 3 44. 8 45. 19 46. 4 47. 50 48. 64

49. 20 50. 22 51. 20 52. 16 53. 90 54. 79 55. 9 56. 78

57. 43 58. 11 59. 22 60. 7 61. 13 62. 12 63. 46 64. 49

65. 8 66. 23 67. 38 68. 92

Page 35: Operations with Mixed Numbers

1. 72/85 2. 3 3/5 3. 2 51/56 4. 14

5. 2 5/6

6. 6 9/10

7. 144/385

8. 2 4/9

9. 3 7/10

10. 25 15/28

11. 21/47

12. 13 9/20

13. 21 3/5

14. 18 13/21

15. 2 44/45

16. 13 5/18

17. 10 1/6

18. 6 3/40

19. 14/51

20. 17 1/9

21. 15 55/56

22. 7/10

23. 73 26/45

24. 57 4/5

25. 8 9/10

26. 3 17/18

27. 3/28

28. 16 1/6

29. 52/245

30. 15

31. 19/40

32. 9 11/12

33. 350/531

34. 5 7/10

35. 7/15

36. 60 2/3

37. 7 32/63

38. 14 67/72

39. 1/10

40. 3 31/42

41. 15 5/9

42. 17 1/10

43. 11 9/40

44. 8 1/14

45. 1 1/6

46. 2 1/4

47. 1 53/90

48. 2 34/35

49. 9 17/24

50. 16 1/6

51. 4 1/15

52. 12 7/8

53. 2 1/25

54. 161/171

55. 17/18

56. 88 22/35

57. 1/6

58. 14 17/20

59. 1/4

Page 47: Multiple Operations with Fractions

1. 51/70

2. 1/12

3. 1 28/45

4. 1 49/72

5. 1

6. 29/90

7. 1/54

8. -19/60

9. 2 29/60

10. 1/10

11. 125/384

12. 83/140

13. 19/40

14. 4/5

15. 0

16. 1 17/24

17. 0

18. 1 53/60

19. 1 11/18

20. 2

21. -1/18

22. 3/8

23. 1/24

24. 1 77/120

25. 1 13/72   26. 1 257/280   27. 1 481/1260   28. 25/108

29. 2/15   30. 1 1/4   31. 0   32. 2 13/40

33. 3/160   34. 5/36   35. 2/15   36. 1 127/140

37. 1/6   38. 1 1/3   39. 1 39/70   40. 2 31/120

41. 1 55/126   42. 533/840   43. 1 19/60   44. 4/15

45. 5/6   46. 2 1/30   47. 1 113/168   48. 11/24

49. 1 5/6   50. 1 7/18   51. 3/32   52. 2 111/280

53. 1 7/9   54. 29/40   55. 4/5   56. 10/27

57. 5/168   58. 3/160   59. 9/98   60. 3/70